It's very seldom that you read a first-time author's book and feel an immediate connection because the content, style, and chemistry of the author reflects that of an experienced veteran writer, but such is the work of Ms. Tonya Thomas. Some may consider it to be very direct in details, and perhaps graphic in nature, but one thing for sure, this riveting nonfiction story will literally have you on the edge of your seat, as she describes in detail the many difficult choices and challenges she faced, yet how her faith has helped her, and continues to help her to fulfill her purpose!

The Detroit native reveals the uncovered truth concerning her childhood struggles, family relationships, pain and rejection, personal decisions, and the unfortunate tragic death of her beloved son. This book, which is appropriately titled, will encourage its readers to seek the real truth, which is the word of God, to walk in the knowledge of truth, forgiveness, and to love and pray for your enemies.

Pastor J. Keith Vincent
Senior Pastor - Greater Compassion

I take great honor in forwarding this book on behalf of Tonya M. Thomas, of whom I serve as her Pastor. Although throughout the years of ministry this strong woman of faith, has shown herself to have great character, a servant's heart, effective communicator, as a well-respected leader and have been a blessing to our church, Mount Zion Baptist church and the Nashville community. With her tremendous heart for the disadvantaged and service of an array of programs, she can now add to her repertoire, author.

She is a woman of relentless strength and tenacity that was more evident as she encounters the greatest challenge known to man, the loss of her only child.

This woman of faith has taken her tragedy and have become triumph in and through it all. By taking her life experiences and writing a story of persevering through adversity and loss to find life and hope. And now she's sharing what she has learned along her journey with others so they can uncover life's truths and be set free in Christ.

Tonya is transparent in telling her story of how she has survived many challenges. In each situation, she explores the lies and betrayals she encountered and then offers the truth that set her free. Although it often takes great courage to tell the truth, she has stepped up to do just that in this remarkable book.

Bishop Joseph W. Walker, III
Senior Pastor- Mount Zion Baptist Church

Am I Your Enemy Because I Tell You the Truth?

By

TONYA M. THOMAS

AM I YOUR ENEMY BECAUSE I TELL YOU THE TRUTH?
Copyright © 2016 by Tonya M. Thomas

All rights reserved. No part of this book may be reproduced (except for inclusion in reviews), disseminated or utilized in any form or by any means, electronic or mechanical, including photocopying, recording, or in any information storage and retrieval system, or the Internet/World Wide Web without written permission from the author or publisher. For permission requests, write to the publisher, addressed: "Attention: Permissions Coordinator," at the address below.

C.O.K Enterprise/Tonya M. Thomas
PO Box 383 Antioch, TN 37011
/http://becauseitellyouthetruth.com

Ordering information: Quantity sales. Special discounts are available on quantity purchases by corporations, associations, and others. For details, contact the "Special Sales Department" at the address above.

Book Cover design by:
C.T. Graphics

Book Layout by:
Dynamark Graphics

ISBN 978-0-9861610

Printed in the United States of America

1. Title 2. Author 3. Fiction

Dedicated
to
Mr. Calvin A. Thomas
&
Mr. Clinton Hall Senior

You both are the wings beneath my wings...
I soar because of you.

AM I YOUR ENEMY BECAUSE I TELL YOU THE TRUTH?

This book serves as a series of a compilation of the human experiences that life brings and requires an answer. This volume I of the 9 volumes are set to take every reader with every circumstance imaginable to the common need of the soul that hungers and thirst for the undeniable thirst quenching and satisfying... Truth.

While it is a fact that life can often bring some horrific and challenging experiences, it is still the choices that we make that can bring change that will ultimately set our lives on different travels.

This is why **quality** choices are so necessary to make for a **permanent** quality and healthy change for a better life.

Life truly is 10% what happens to you and 90% how you react to it" ...Charles R. Swindoll

We can never get away from hurt, pain, and disappointment there seems to never be an escape from any of it, you have to know though it really came to ...pass, it was never meant to stay. When what's in front of you become more important than what was behind you will indeed have the escape you both yearn for and are deserving of.

You can set for a healthy and abundant life while taking every lesson from these would-be challenges and by escaping the webs and chains of the lie and being and remaining set free because of truth.

The choice is yours, do you want to be better or bitter?

Tonya M. Thomas

Contents

Preface 1
Introduction 5

Chapter 1
The Truth Begins With You 9

Chapter 2
From Victim to Victor 69

Chapter 3
Be Yourself Because Everyone Else Is Already Taken 91

Chapter 4
To Learn From the Past Is the Wisdom of the Future 103

Chapter 5
Truth Should Be Understood and Lived to Bear Fruit 141

Chapter 6
Wherever You Put Your Energy, That's What You Energize 165

Chapter 7
Places of Worship: Lifelines or Shipwrecks? 179

Chapter 8
God's Specific Blessings Made With You in Mind 209

Chapter 9
Are You Satisfied or Pacified? 253

Chapter 10
Forgiveness The Final Frontier 265

ABOUT THE AUTHOR 270

PREFACE

As a master Potter, a genius Scientist, and a visionary Developer, God always had you in mind and had you in His hands. But you might be saying, "Now wait just a minute, Tonya. You couldn't possibly believe a loving Father God would allow me to go through what I have been through in my life and call it good!" But believe me. It's true! I can only humbly speak to you from my own experience and thoughts and those I've observed of others, and this is what I will share with you throughout this book.

For me, the biblical story that best illustrates the solemn place and rest I'm experiencing now is the story of the potter in the Book of Jeremiah (Jeremiah 18:1-6). When I read this passage, the word that gets my attention is arise (verse 2). In my darkest seasons, I had to get up and out of the slums of depression, mediocrity, and apathy and tell myself, *There has to be more than this in life.* But the most important part for me is when the prophet says he "went down to the potter's house" (verse 3). *Going down* speaks of humility because the truth is that I don't have all the answers, nor am I required to.

My travels have taken me throughout the United States and abroad. On a tour of Germany and Istanbul , Turkey, I saw an array of art that was simply mind-blowing with its beautiful colors and designs. Though I saw masterful paintings, glasswork, and other works of art, my favorite display was the pottery. While traveling in Cappadocia, I experienced the process of a master potter, which brought home to me the life-changing passage in Jeremiah.

While watching a demonstration by a master potter, I was chosen from the audience to participate in making a piece of pottery. I had never made pottery before, but Cappadocia is a country known best for beautiful pottery, so I embraced the opportunity to be trained by a master.

The first thing the potter taught me was that I needed to adjust my posture as I sat down at the wheel. My posture had to be strong and firm, with my back straight (which spoke to me of the boldness and confidence of God, the Potter, who has the authority and power). Next, my feet had to be in position to tap the wheel's pedal (which represents how adversities are allowed to tap my will into proper alignment with God's will). To me, the wheel was symbolic of my own will that had to be tapped to put it in constant alignment to the Potter so His divine work can be completed.

The clay I worked with was carefully chosen by the potter. As soon as I held it in my hands I noticed how cold and hard it was. It was also marred. Like the clay, I too was marred, being entrapped with the lies of life. The clay was messy, and to make it more pliable, I had to use a constant stream of water. This reminded me of how the Holy Spirit and the Word of God work on me to

Am I Your Enemy Because I Tell You The Truth?

We are the clay
You are the potter
We are all the work of Your hands

Isaiah 64:8

make me more useful for His service. The more water that was used, the more the clay changed. But I still had to stretch it and remove pieces that no longer served the purpose of the design I had in mind.

I thought about my life and how I have had some serious hits and stretching, but I know that if I didn't have those hits and times of stretching, I would have stayed in places I should not have been in; held on to relationships I shouldn't have been in; held onto ideologies, methodologies, and behavior patterns that would not have moved me closer to me destiny. And there have been people I had to walk away from who had become excess in my life because they were not part of the God's masterful design for my life.

Tonya M. Thomas

But through the turning of the wheel and the warmth of my hands, the clay began to form a recognizable image. I had to remember all the things the potter had taught me, and the clay had to stay in my hands, but I saw what that piece of pottery would become, and it was beautiful!

My brothers and sisters, we are in God's hands. Though there are moments when it seems that life is full of challenges, roughness, and constant disappointment, don't worry. The end result of God's masterpiece is turning into something so beautiful. The miracle you is evolving into the destined you that you were always supposed to become!

INTRODUCTION

The lip of truth shall be established forever, but a lying tongue is but for a moment.—-Proverbs 12:19

Has someone ever looked you in the eye, without blinking, and told you something that was so far from the truth that you immediately recognized that they lying to you and to themselves, too? We live in a world where lies have become the norm, and truth has become abnormal. Goodness, kindness, and courtesy are rare attributes. In the political arena, character assassination and mudslinging have taken the place of honesty, commitment, and integrity as the path to good leadership.

The days of choosing a spouse, being faithful, and raising a family have been replaced by single-parenting as a viable option. Alternative lifestyles and same-sex marriages are labeled "the new norm."

There was a time when the police and the judicial system were well respected, but no longer. They brought order to our society, not disorder. Whatever happened to protect and serve?

Impressionable youth grew up having aspirations of becoming something and playing significant roles in society. Boys wanted to be firemen, doctors, racecar drivers, lawyers, and athletes, or they wanted to go into the military. Girls wanted to be ladies and grow up to be teachers, nurses, secretaries, and nurturing mothers instead of hardened, callous women competing with men to see who can be the most macho.

What happened to our churches? They used to be havens of refuge where people could get good, sound Bible teaching. But now they're just social clubs that can function whether the Holy Spirit shows up or not.

Reality television replaced good old-fashioned television. At one time, trained, passionate studio actors performed appropriate storylines with great skill. There used to be shows the whole family could enjoy together. But now we see shows with high crime, demonic and dark imagery, illicit sexual content that could be made as porn, and stories that promote lies and deceit—all while desensitizing our very moral fiber. You would be surprised to know all the ill effects of the subliminal messages that come through these outlets that serve only to promote and perpetuate poor lifestyles choices.

I never thought in writing this book that I would be opening myself up to the enemy and his lynch mob. But anytime you stand for truth and threaten to expose a system that breeds, grooms, perpetrates, and thrives off of lies, then you become public enemy number one. Depending on how much of a threat you are against a system will determine the measure of the force the enemy will send against you.

So what qualifies me to make such statements? What qualifies me to take such a stand? Because I know God's Word.

Am I Your Enemy Because I Tell You The Truth?

I have been lied on, ostracized, and destitute, and I've been homeless. I've been betrayed by family members, pastors, and church members, leaving so many knives in my back that you couldn't even see me anymore, what was most devastating was who held the handles. Sometimes I had more love and loyalty from the streets, from the unlearned and the unchurched, than I ever received from people who claimed to love me.

There were times I was without so long that it became my new normal. I've been robbed and abandoned; and I've survived broken relationships, divorce, the death a child, health challenges, broken dreams, and molestation.

I've made permanent decisions on temporary circumstances and was bankrupt spiritually, financially, morally, mentally, and emotionally. And I have been put out of churches, family liaisons, jobs, and homes. So what qualifies me is that after going through these horrific challenges because of lies that were told, I have survived.

When you stand for truth like I have, you will find yourself loved and hated, often with the same intensity. I have gone through many levels of hell and snatched all the necessary keys to, first, unlock myself and then, second, to free as many other people as I could. Never go through hell and not get the keys. Just as Jesus went through the doors of death and hell took the keys so we can be free, so now I can say, "Death is swallowed up in victory. O death, where is thy sting? O grave, where is thy victory? (1 Corinthians 15:54-55).

Tonya M. Thomas

Although this book could be considered a self-help book, actually its foundation of transforming healing and deliverance is all accredited to our Lord and Savior, Jesus Christ. Jesus said of His Word, "If ye continue in my word, then are ye my disciples indeed; and ye shall know the truth, and the truth shall make you free" (John 8:31-32). And of His Son, He said, "If the Son therefore shall make you free, ye shall be free indeed" (John 8:36). And since the Word is God and God is Truth, you can't help but be blessed by His Word.

Self-help books alone can leave you inspired, but a book that uses the Word of God and His strategies will leave you forever changed, for how can anything have meaning, substance, and consistency if truth is not its foundation? If you don't open yourself to the life of the light of truth, you will forever remain in the dark. This is a race for your destiny, so stop wasting time, and run toward your destiny.

Am I your enemy because I tell you the truth?

CHAPTER 1
The Truth Begins With You

When discovered, who you are will introduce you to the truth.

"And last of all he was seen of me also, as of one born out of due time. But by the grace of God I am what I am"
(1 Corinthians 15:8, 10).

Who Are You?

After Jesus' temptation in the wilderness (Luke 4), He entered the synagogue and read the Scriptures to those who were gathered. They were so amazed by His words that they asked, "Is not this Joseph's son?" (verse 22).

If someone were to question who you are, what would you answer? I can assure you that the answer won't be found in your clothes, charisma, intellect, finances, pedigree, or career. In fact, those things often misrepresent you and don't tell the whole story of who you are.

Perhaps the men in the synagogue were asking a rhetorical question. Jesus had grown up in Nazareth, so surely they knew who He was and that Joseph was His earthly father. Instead of answering their question about his origin, however, Jesus spoke to them of deeper truths, which angered (verse 28) and astonished them "because his word was with power" (verse 32).

Tonya M. Thomas

Jesus knew that the people who questioned His identity had limited foresight and knowledge. Many times when people witness miraculous things, they have no point of reference, so they find it hard to accept and believe the truth of what happened. Instead of accepting the truth, they try to bring you down to their small and limited thinking.

Perhaps that's why the people asked, "Is not this Joseph's son?" as if to say that Jesus wasn't anything special; He was just a carpenter's son from the local village.

Although people might be touched and affected by you, they perceive you as a threat because you've challenged them in ways they would rather not be challenged. Their refusal to acknowledge the truth breeds contempt.

People who experience the truth of you can't quite figure you out. You are out of the box and challenge their preconceived notions. According to their system and design, you are out of order. So instead of being embraced as a miracle and accepted into the fold, often you will be rejected and abused. But as your life unfolds and is revealed, they won't be able to deny that you are chosen.

I am the greatest. I said that even before I knew I was.
--Muhammad Ali

As human beings, our physical features and attributes point to our families—immediate families as well as more distant relatives. If you met my father, you would know that he is my biological father. From my height to my lips to my facial structure, you

Am I Your Enemy Because I Tell You The Truth?

would see my father's attributes. But while my father is physically handsome and I was fortunate enough to inherit his features, it is the attributes of my true Father, the Lord Jesus Christ, like my eyes and smile, that not only turns people's heads, but those same attributes cause people to stop and marvel. There are times when they look at me in total amazement and often stay to take another look.

The Bible says that the people in the synagogue fastened their eyes on Jesus. His words were so powerful that they "[bared] him witness and wondered at the gracious words which proceeded out of his mouth" (verse 22).

The most amazing thing about being a child of the King is that you will always leave a witness. The Greek word for "witness" is *martooreh*, which means "to testify or to bear record of what one has seen, heard, or known." Jesus testified to who He was by His Spirit through signs and miracles. We also testify to who we are through the manifestation of the Spirit in our lives.

In writing about the differences between your spiritual and natural attributes, I am not criticizing your parents or challenging your relationship with them. I am simply encouraging you to look beyond the surface of who you think you are, or who other people think you are, and explore a deeper truth.

Many of you were blessed to have had unselfish, loving, nurturing, protective, and healthy parents. I didn't have that growing up, but the Lord allowed me to be a healthy parent for my own son. So I'm proof that even if you didn't grow up in a loving and caring environment, which is a grave catastrophe for those of us who endured it, it did not nor ever will stop your true Father from being the Father you deserve and should have.

For many people who didn't have parents who gave them good role models, they find themselves disadvantaged when it comes to self-development, physical awareness (inherited health issues), generational habits, cultivated mindsets, self-defeating and self-sabotaging behaviors, and misuse and abuse acceptance from others. They were not told who they are, therefore they have been misguided or mislead about their true identity.

But when it comes to my spiritual DNA, I know exactly who I am. If you watch *The Maury Show*, you know that his guests often are looking to confirm or deny the paternity of their children. If I were to go on Maury's show to find out the identity of my spiritual Father, Maury would have no other choice but to open the envelope and say emphatically to my natural father, "No, you are not the father!" To be perfectly honest, I would probably leap for joy and dance across the stage, saying, "I knew it! I knew it!"

Let your heavenly Father tell you who you are. People cannot tell you who you are. Don't allow your value to be placed in the hands of people, they can change their minds moments by moment. They cannot validate you; people are dealing with hurts, insecurities, dysfunction of their own and they can project that on you. If allowed you can internalize the hurt from hurting people who can tell you lies. "You are not worthy, you are ugly, you don't deserve to be loved, "you will only get their approval or affirmation if you dance to their song, the challenge is their beats too often change. You and I did not come from our parents but rather through our parents. God calls you His masterpiece, the apple of His eye, and His beloved. Everything about you from your height, color, hair, built, the way you think, your creative style, all sets you apart and was perfected for the original design of you. You are not a knock-off but an original. The longer you walk in the unknown as to who you are, you will continually be what "they" want you to be, act the way "they want you to act, and compromise your extraordinary self to a discounted rack at good will because you became "they will" as oppose to the "will of Christ.

"He predestined us for adoption to son ship through Jesus Christ, in accordance with his pleasure and will"
—Eph. 1:5 NIV

Everything God made was good and he already said you are fearfully and wonderfully made, so do me and you a favor, yes right now. Look into the mirror and look at that masterpiece that's reflecting back at you. Yesssssss really look, it's amazing isn't it "Now say to that original design that is looking back at you, "you are wonderful, marvelous, and totally amazing, and I love you. You may have been like me, most of my life I can admire, take care of, appreciate everyone else design and not love mines enough. Now go back and answer that question and let them know who you are and say it as with your shoulders tall, backbone strong, and as my brother Kevin Hart will say "with your chest sticking out", emphatically" I AM A CHILD OF THE KING".

Destiny

The world and I applaud your presence. Your birth was divinely planned already. God, the crafted Potter and genius Scientist, is a visionary developer and always had you in mind.

From the moment you're born, you're headed toward your destiny. When one of your father's sperm won the race to your mother's egg, you came into being; but the fight to win didn't stop there. Now that you're here, you have to fight each day along the journey to your destiny.

There are two important times in a man's life:
the day of his birth and the day he discovers his purpose.
––Mark Twain

By definition, *destiny* is "what happens in the future, the events someone will experience in the future, a power that is believed to control what happens in the future." So everything, from the surrounding culture, your background, your community, and even your family can be so off-kilter that it can prevent you from knowing who you are and what your destiny is.

To stay on course, you must know the truth about who you are. Who you are is not limited to where you came from, though this information can give you more insight as to who you came through and why you are here. When you understand what is in you, it will

Am I Your Enemy Because I Tell You The Truth?

become clear that what is in you has prepared you for who you are and who you will become.

I admire the great world evangelist James Robinson. Robinson has touched the lives of so many people all over the world with the Word of God, he has ministered to their natural needs as well with food, water, and clothing. You might never guess that Robinson was the product of rape. Though his beginning was fraught with pain and shame, Robinson has turned his circumstances into a life lived to minister to others the love of Jesus Christ.

Experts might have predicted quite a different end for a man born into such circumstances. They might have suggested that Robinson would continue the cycle of dysfunction by becoming a rapist or, even worse, a murderer.

Like many children conceived through rape, Robinson probably wouldn't have been born. After all, how many women would choose to be raped by a stranger, experiencing such horrific physical, emotional, and spiritual pain only to be further reminded of her experience by giving birth to a child who might resemble the predator or, even worse, have his same twisted characteristics? Try explaining that at the family reunion, at the child's daycare, or at Sunday school! How could she help her child to understand who and where his father was, and how would she explain to her child about his other side of the family? What would this child grow up to be? What would be his destiny?

Yet Robinson not only survived, despite his natural father's violent act, but he has thrived because of what his heavenly Father has done in his life. The Lord promised that He is a father to the fatherless, and when His seed (Word) is planted in you, you will not only look like Him, but you will carry his attributes in what you do and in what you say.

While my father side has strong genes. I don't have many of my mother's genes. My mother Mrs. Delores Eileen Thomas however, is very beautiful she has the look of a goddess? Her incredible features and beautiful skin is beyond words. She also is a very creative woman and has the ability of taking less and making more. She is very strong though, life has thrown her its shares of many challenges

My mother married young with my father and did not have the opportunity of true self-discovery apart of her relationship with my dad. Beginning that marriage with now both a unplanned pregnancy and a mother who already did not approve of my dad and a host of insecurities that stemmed from unresolved issues and pain was a recipe for "hurting people hurt people". My father certainly had his share of baggage with his insecurities, being a tall skinny dark-skin man with bi-focals, although he made it cool internally he suffered. There were many hidden hurts and insecurities that dwelt with him one in particular that scarred and wounded him and became a strong part of his pain was the learning of the truth about his father. My grandmother did not disclose his true father, and he had learned about it in the most devastating way. That lie like all lies will always find a way to surface, unfortunately no one will ever be prepared for it and all its ill effects. For a man particularly

Am I Your Enemy Because I Tell You The Truth?

being a leader by expectation, finds it even more hard and complex not to at least have a starting point, as to where he began. My father will later be hell on wheels and like the Tasmanian devil anything and anyone he touches are subject to his terror. My mother longed for his love and will do anything to get it, I don't believe my father never knew what love was and thereby never being able to give it. I often say "people can only spend what's in their purse." Though both my parents do have their individual strengths, creativity, and smarts it was their pain that they worked out of when it came to me and my siblings. But their need of approval especially for image sake to other family members, public, neighbors, and other organization would be the only consistent and rewarding affirmation that they sought and worked hard for, even at the expense of their own children. This selfishness would cause the grave dysfunction that I and my siblings would endure. Having survived my household, still did not deflect God's hand on my life.

Destiny has a way of revealing itself in strange and sometimes hurting places. Some indicators are what moves you, provokes anger, stirs your passion, and sets you apart with no reference.

Those who understand the Spirit often tell me that I have my Father's eyes and smile, which tells me that my spiritual DNA comes directly from my heavenly Father. I am told that I can see right through a person. The truth is I often see their soul and the state it's in. These two attributes alone separate me from the norm, placing me on a unique and different path.

Tonya M. Thomas

Now God, being the greatest Creator and Strategist there is, knew in His divine plan that I would have the parents I have. While I proudly share their attributes, they don't define my destiny.

God's plan for my destiny is at work because He knows all things. While He allows us to choose our mates, neighbors, friends, and employment he doesn't allow us to choose our biological families. But despite how good or how bad the environment we grew up in, God uses our circumstances ultimately for our good. When you realize that the events of your life have been predetermined and that there is nothing and no one else that can keep you from your destiny, you will than have a sense of rest. However, what can delay your destiny is when you are unable to identify the truth of who you are and when you rely on substandard tools and people for answers. In other words, it is your responsibility and yours alone to get to know intimately the incredible you that you are; and the only way to begin this journey and know all of its truths is through our Creator, our Lord Jesus Christ.

Otherwise you will place your value and your need of affirmation through people. Your value does not come from people it comes from the most High God. Yes, it may hurt at times that you did not get the validation you deserved, before you lose another second trying to get the approval of your family, friends, coworkers google your manufacture, the Lord Jesus Christ.

To know these truths, you will need a Bible, the Word of God. Choose a version that is suitable for you Kings James, New

Am I Your Enemy Because I Tell You The Truth?

International, a study Bible, for examples and get into His Word. Study it, and meditate on it.

You don't have to be a strong church member (the organization) or a Bible scholar to study God's Word (the organism). I'm not telling you not to go to church or to try to learn as much as you can. I'm saying that reading and digesting God's Word will plant His seeds in your life, which will help you to form a relationship with God, which is the most important aspect of reading the Word. After forming this relationship, you will begin to see His attributes in your life.

When I first began to study this gem of a book, I wasn't as interested in church. I was in desperate need of trying to learn me and why was I so different, I not only not fit in with peers, school mates, even certain family members I just had this need to be emancipate from this void I needed to know my manufacture. I then learned more about God. The Word is God (John 1:1). But I found that relying on any book other than the Bible, would be the same as when women rely on women's magazines or social media articles (which are usually written by other women) to understand how men think. Instead of relying on questionable tools to help you gain important information, go to the source. If you want to know about men, how they think or what they like, it's probably best to talk to men. If someone wants to know more about you, he or she would do themselves a disservice by relying on some other source or talking to anyone other than you.

Although I appreciate many great people, positive thinkers, and rich and affluent scholars of many sorts and the knowledge they possess, they all like me, were created by God. So when I need information beyond what I know or what others know, I believe in relying solely on God, the Source and the Creator of all things. Because he knows that timing and preparation are uniquely tied to your destiny, the enemy will distract you with time stealers, those things that keep you from your season, from joy, and from God's rich blessings. The enemy knows he can't ultimately stop God's plan for your life, but he will do anything to distract you and at the very least cause you to be unprepared for your destiny. Timing and preparation are essential for giving birth to your destiny. These twin powers will always precede God's many miracles and revelations in your life. This is why you will have to learn to guard your time and always allow for preparation as it is predestined, or predetermined, for you to be victorious, to win, and always triumph.

The Enemy Is an Identity Thief
If you're struggling with understanding your identity and walking in your destiny, don't be discouraged. When I started writing this book, I never thought the enemy would attack me to no end. But I learned that anytime we come against a system and attempt to proclaim truth, the devil will attack us; and once we're on his hit list, we become public enemy number one! The bigger you are as

Am I Your Enemy Because I Tell You The Truth?

a threat to the enemy's lies, the more force he will send to take you out.

Now that I've been on this journey to proclaim truth, I have become well acquainted with the enemy and his cohorts and all their ranks. But I'm not worried about it because the Scripture encourages me that I can do all things through Christ who strengthens me. In fact, I'm encouraged by the enemy's attacks.

By attacking me, the enemy confirms who I am and, more importantly, whose I am. My stock must be pretty high for me to be on the enemy's radar like this. No one sends out an army to take out someone who is wimpy, weak, and nonthreatening. The mere fact that I am met with such hostility by the enemy is a great indicator of the gift I possess and the purpose that is on my life.

The devil wages war to take us into bondage and keep us there, and he never fights a fair fight. But never forget that he is a defeated foe, and God has already condemned him to an eternity of damnation. Because the devil already knows his fate, he's trying to take as many people with him as he can.

Even in our families, the enemy fights to steal our identities, causing a ripple effect of dysfunction and pain. My parents fought bitterly and cheated on each other regularly. As a child, I couldn't understand why. As an adult, I learned that my parents only got married because my mother was pregnant with me. As I learned more about my parents and why they made the decisions they did, I discovered that they had led empty and unfulfilled lives because they accepted the lie. They had no true identity and didn't know who they really were supposed to be.

My parents got married because that's what they thought they were supposed to do, whether or not that was the right decision for them or for me. My parents were still trying to grow up themselves and discover their identities. Instead, they were stuck in a loveless marriage with children they regretted having too soon, and we all paid dearly for their decision.

And now I'd like to address how important it is that you, men and women, consider carefully before sharing your precious God-given gift––your bodies. Looking closely at the human body, our design and purpose become clearer.

Men, you were designed to be givers, not receivers. With your testicles, you write your testaments. Women, you were designed to be receivers, not givers. You are an open book filled with blank pages, for every time you open your legs, you open your book. You must be careful who you allow to write in on the pages of your books. If some women had to choose a genre for their books, they would have to choose horror, drama, romance mystery, action and adventure, satire, science fiction, or "Somebody Help Me!"

Men, I like to refer to you as kings because you are the heads, the leaders, the chiefs, the captains, and the forerunners of your kingdoms, and I honor all of you who lead well. You must be selective of the women who carry your seed, your testament, and your story. Those of you who have allowed the boy in you to drive your lives have had so many books written that the Library of

Am I Your Enemy Because I Tell You The Truth?

Congress cannot contain them all! Then you have the audacity to be upset at the "friend of the court office," the many children you have to take care of, the drama and the horror stories of the books you've chosen to write in.

My brothers, my kings, you should choose wisely and stop letting the boy in you drive your lives. Instead, you should let the king in you get out of riding shotgun and lead you to your promised land where you can write your own history.

My brothers/kings, when making these intentional and divine decisions, first ask yourself, *What kind of story would I like to leave behind?* It is your story or the lack thereof that causes many of you to suffer because you're never quite sure what your identity is. It's what you said or didn't say that has our world in much of its chaos.

You have to realize that the power you possess is shaping our families, communities, and our world. So be careful of what you're texting, tweeting, saying, and doing. God said, "Let there be," and whatever He said came into being. He gave you the same authority, because your power of words or the lack thereof is suffering our society. Speak man! tells us when we are wrong but please tell us when we are right. Speak men! speak life in us it's never how much you say or great use of the vocabulary, it's what you say. The women, children, world are waiting on your voice to activate us to our destiny. We are dying of thirst and lacking air of life because of the lack of your words.

Tonya M. Thomas

The keys of truth is in your mouth to unlock the chains of bondages in our lives. We need *you* **Man** you are the head, leaders, creators, the first. The only revolution we really need is the revelation of you and your existence in our lives, don't take another word to the grave that you should have given to us.

You hold the keys to this world not the government, church, schools, and communities; for without you it's no us. We need you, we want you, and we LOVE you. We don't care what mistakes you've made, repent and come back, please, our hearts and doors are awaiting the key of you to come in for only you have. The welcome mat is and will always be there, we miss you. There is nothing we can't get through together, You are already forgiven, and yes we will follow you lead.

Remember, destruction didn't befall mankind because Eve ate a piece of fruit. It was when Adam ate the fruit. Adam could have and should have ignored Eve's enticing request to eat the fruit. I'm sure he could have gotten another woman, too, provided that he didn't fall. But, instead, he listened to Eve, ate the fruit, and brought the curse of sin upon the human race. Many of our great kings have fallen because of a "piece". I could interview them today, they would have to admit that the "piece" wasn't worth it!

For you my sisters, my queens, you are the most important piece in the world. Like chess pieces in motion, you can make the same moves that your king can make, only more so. Which is why it's true that women mature faster than men do. That's not to say that women are necessarily smarter than men, just a bit quicker. You

Am I Your Enemy Because I Tell You The Truth?

are not the sum total of your relationships. Please note though before you are a girlfriend, wife, mother you are a woman love yourself first so that you will not have to be at the mercy of those who won't.

Women, it is highly important that you know your value. You and I know that that clearance racks and sales draw all people. When you discount your value you can and will draw anything and everything. Stop giving men discounts, for low prices (low living) attracts customers. Your clothing, attitude, countenance, are all languages what are you really saying?

Let me remind you of the power you possess: Every human being in the world must come through a woman. So I ask to you my queens, What are you birthing in this world? What are you allowing to come into existence? What are you contributing to our society that is rocking our world? Remember, it's your hands that rock the cradle of our society.

As women, two of the most honorable unique roles we fill include our ability to be "womb-men" and mothers. We don't fill these roles just for our own children, though. A woman (man with a womb) is a walking womb, which is a place where something or someone is generated. This place is not limited to the birth of children. It can also birth ideas, methodologies, programs, and the why's of why things occur.

This is why women, in all our creative attributes, have the greatest ability to regenerate. Because of that, we have to guard, protect, and be ever so humbly conscious about what we allow to come in to us, and we have to be even more careful about what goes out. As women, we can use our creative talents and then take almost anything to heights unknown. Which is why a man can purchase a house, but only a woman can make it a home.

It's what she puts in it that gives it life and grandeur. She can make it a beautiful, healthy home inside and out. Her husband and children will feel the love by what she filled it with—peace, motivation, encouragement, safe boundaries, and care.

Her eyes light up when her family comes in because she knows they can see and feel her love, which carries over into each of their lives at work, at school, and wherever they go. She leaves a legacy of love that her children can carry into adulthood and perpetuate with their own children.

On the other hand, a foolish woman will tear down her home with her own hands. Her family will feast on diets of wickedness, gossip, anger, and insecurity. The foolish woman's family will die under her control because in her presence they are broken and hopeless. She has filled her home with hostility, lies, strife, and prejudices.

She doesn't nurture and nourish. She manipulates and controls. Her poisonous actions bleeds over into everything they do at work, at school, and anywhere else they go. The foolish woman's legacy is rage and insecurity, and she sets up children to perpetuate it for generations.

God has given women a most precious responsibility, so be careful how you handle it. The greatest power in the world is to

Am I Your Enemy Because I Tell You The Truth?

carry and bring forth life. Carrying life is the ultimate calling, so women are the doors of life. The greatest human beings on the planet all had one thing in common: They all came from a wombman—even Jesus Christ Himself. Which even the more I honor you. Rather you birth a child and raised them yourselves or birth and gave them to be raised by someone else, I honor you. Not all mothers are nurtures but they are to yet be respected the same. I myself personally, had to come to the conclusion that while my mother was qualified to birth me she was not qualified to raise me and that was fine. I respect her all the same for her willingness to carry me and birth and for that I am eternally grateful of her and I honor her. Some women may not physically birth children but they birth them spiritually and emotionally I honor you for you were well qualified for the task.

From the beginning of Creation, there was a strategic and intentional assault set forth for women.

And I will put enmity between thee and the woman and between thy seed and her seed. Gen. 3:15

The perfect hatred that the enemy has toward women is beyond words, This evil is past your understanding. This is why so many women have the constant battle of the enemy attempting to plant his seeds of chaos in their lives. From jealousies, insecurities, gossips, and sowing discord, many women find themselves the conduits of such acts that has destroyed many relationships, organizations, communities, churches, and schools that they can both birth and nurtured it. The enemy being a polished and astute soldier knows that to do permanent damage to win a war, you go where your opponent has its greatest strength. The greatest strength for the human race is its ability to reproduce of its own kind. This is why all lives matter.

You don't have to believe the lie the enemy tells you. You are who God says you are, not who society tells you you should be. The decisions you make now will affect you and many others for years to come, so stand up to the enemy and take back your identity!

As you and I fight our battles, we must always remember that "greater is He that is in [us] than he that is in the world." Be assured that our God has equipped us for it all, and we need it because "the weapons of our warfare are not carnal, but mighty through God to the pulling down of strong holds" (2 Corinthians 10:4).

So arm yourself with the weapons God has provided for you: God's Word, the name of Jesus, the cross, the blood of Jesus, worship, and peace. Use these weapons to fight the enemy at every turn. Don't let him steal your identity and make you forget who you are. Remember, you belong to Christ, and you're already on the winning side!

Finding Truth in Exile

The greatest quest for your life's journey is finding, understanding, and accepting the most important gift: your life. This quest will require serious soul-searching and might be the most difficult task you will ever endure, but it will be the most rewarding.

Am I Your Enemy Because I Tell You The Truth?

You first have to accept that in your genuine uniqueness you will not always see a point of reference in your family or around you. In some cases, you will find similarities and familiarities within some of these places. Your background, family, and education are often just conduits that have brought you to a particular place, but these things don't completely define the wonderful you that you are.

If you don't know who you are and what you possess, you will always find yourself in a place prescribed by what others think you should become. Never allow the standards of the world to dictate to you who you should become. From radio to television-"telling their vision", all have continually demonstrated their unreliable and unhealthy practices that have led to destructive life-styles. From unhealthy marriages, drug abuse, and self-afflicted behaviors. If you and I were really able to see the backdrop of these alluring props you will immediately discover the "lies".

While others might have our best interest at heart, many times we open ourselves to the will of others. After seeking to please them, we're left with moments of absolute nothing, leaving us an empty shell nomadically searching but never coming to a place of solace. It's most amazing that a lie can run all around your life, family, church, school, and community before truth has put its shoes on.

Truth doesn't have to be validated.--Dick Gregory

The apostle John was banished to the isle of Patmos because he preached the gospel of Jesus Christ. Patmos, a sterile and desolate place, was a prison island, and exiled people were sent there as punishment. But even in the midst of this desolate place, God revealed the Book of Revelation to John, and he saw heavenly visions. In Greek, the word translated as "revelation" is *apocalypses* and means "to take the cover off." For John, his time on Patmos allowed him to see the unveiling of Christ's glory and other future events.

I have been through my own personal "Patmos time," a period of time when I was alone and quiet. During this season, I was able to be still and experience God's revelation power in my life. It was in these still, quiet periods that the cover of lies was removed, and my destiny was made clearer to me.

If you're experiencing Patmos time, don't despair. This is a strategic time planned by God. While you might experience the death of old habits and ways of thinking, you will also be reborn and experience a metamorphosis of your new self. It will be you but not the same old you. The saying goes, "There is another man in that man. There is another woman in that woman." This is the type of rebirth and renewal that will happen during your Patmos time.

In some parts of Africa, there is a belief that tribal masks contain spirits, and if a person wears one of those masks, he or she will become that spirit. In our lives, we wear masks sometimes, too. We don't wear wooden masks painted, decorated, and worn for a tribal ritual. Our masks are social and cultural and hide our innermost thoughts and feelings.

Am I Your Enemy Because I Tell You The Truth?

Some of us have worn so many different masks for so many different reasons that we have completely lost sight of who we really are. We have different masks for family members, friends, co-workers, spouses, children, neighbors, strangers, and even for ourselves. Often, we end up confused and frustrated, especially when we forget which mask we're wearing and why.

But when you wear your masks, you convince people you don't need them or their help, even when you really do need help. Because your masks convey a sense of false strength and tell the lie that you have it all together when you don't. God didn't create us to go it alone, but when you wear masks, people can't see the true you, and you create distance between you and everyone else, although you need them and they need you.

So we don't need masks of any kind to hide behind. Instead, we are transformed by the Word of God and are renewed by the Spirit of Christ. When God's Spirit takes precedence in our lives, it will unmask who we are and who we are destined to become. In that way, we will no longer need any type of mask.

Through the Spirit, you can embrace the truth of who you are and drop all masks. You can stand before the Lord and everyone else, completely naked and unashamed, showing your true self.

The greatest purpose of your Patmos time is that there are no distractions from anything or anyone. When you're alone in that place, you can shed the masks you've been hiding behind. You're not plugged in to all the things that would usually pull you in different directions.

Tonya M. Thomas

You also have to realize that other people can't share your Patmos time. God takes you into your desolate place to reveal more of Himself and more of His plan for you. He wants to talk more about His assignment for you. God is a jealous God and will not allow any interruptions or challenges to His divine plan.

Other people would be a distraction during this time. They would not benefit or be able to add anything of value to your time alone with God. You must learn that there are times along your journey when you simply can't take other people to a place they were not qualified or equipped for. You must release them for the time being and bring everything into subjection to God. The release will bring an immediate charge of no return from your former and carry you on to the heights of your new frontier.

You will also discover that the more you embrace truth and become your higher self that the crowd around you will begin to thin out. Think of your life like a pyramid: The higher up you go, the smaller it gets. You will find that the higher you ascend, that crowd of loved ones, friends, associates, and mates will probably dissipate.

Don't be discouraged because you won't be left alone. God will be with you. But there are times that, other than Him, you must learn to be by yourself, learn to like and love yourself, and get in tune with yourself. Then you can ask the tough questions and see how your choices can be clearer and better through the light of the truth.

Living in the Matrix

I was born the ninth day of June, and as my mother often said, "5:49 p.m., 7 pounds and 10 ounces." I didn't just start to exist on June 9; that was just the day I was born. I began to exist the day I was conceived. However, because June 9 is the day I was born, that day is significant.

I don't think of myself as a numerologist of any kind, but I believe the day on which a person makes their entrance into this earthly realm is significant. Since I was born on the ninth day, I've researched the significance of the number 9.

- There are nine fruit of the Spirit (Galatians 5:22-23).
- There are nine planets.
- It takes nine months to form a human being.
- The human body has 9 holes (2 ears, 2 eyes, 2 nostrils, 1 mouth, 1 urethra, 1 anus)
- Nine was the name of the sacred mountain of the sun for ancient Egyptians.
- Nine symbolizes divine completeness or finality. Jesus died at the ninth hour, or 3 p.m. In some religious traditions, there were nine gates that separated the sacred enclosure (the Holy of Holies) from the rest of the temple areas.
- The Day of Atonement (Yom Kipur) is the only annual Jewish feast day that requires Jews to fast. This special day, considered by Jews to be the holiest of the year, begins at sunset on the ninth day of the seventh Hebrew month (Leviticus 23:32).

- Nine was called "the Mother Teresa number" because when she saw injustice and suffering, she devoted herself to rectifying it. More importantly, she didn't try to gain credit for her actions. The purity of the math that was manifested when she added to the lives of others was mirrored in the way she went about it.

Exodus 13:15 says, "And it came to pass, when Pharaoh would hardly let us go, that the Lord slew all the firstborn in the land of Egypt, both the firstborn of man, and the firstborn of beast; therefore I sacrifice to the Lord all that openeth the matrix, being males; but all the firstborn of my children I redeem."

The passage in Exodus mentions the matrix. In Hebrew, *matrix* is *rechem*, which means "womb." This reference reminds me of one of my all-time favorite films, *The Matrix*. Like a few of my other favorite movies, this one was a great depiction of the created us. It contained so many parables, which are earthly expressions and references used to represent spiritual themes.

Neo, the main character, had lived an ordinary life with nothing fulfilling, exciting, or out of the ordinary to happen to him. Then he ate the pill of the truth, after which there was no turning back. He was finally introduced to his true self. From that point on, his journey took him to unprecedented heights with eagle's wings.

There are some profound truths in *The Matrix* that illustrate how to become acquainted with our true selves. When sperm (seed) enters the womb (the matrix), it only seeks to reproduce of its

Am I Your Enemy Because I Tell You The Truth?

own kind. The ultimate quest of *The Matrix* involves Neo, the chosen one, being put in place to prevent unauthorized agents from reproducing their own kind. These enemy agents were assigned to deploy Neo from reaching and completing his assignment.

> *For if you remain silent at this time, relief and deliverance for the Jews will arise from another place, but you and your father's house shall will perish. And who knows whether thou art come to the kingdom for such a time as this? Esther 4:14*

That's not unlike those who oppose us in our own lives. When our enemies realize that they can't beat us, they will often elect to join us in order to carry out their plans. Although it may appear that they are unified with us, they are not. It will only be a matter of time before they put their plan in motion to destroy us.

....They went out from us, that they might be manifest that they were not all of us 1 John 2:19

The agents from *The Matrix* remind me of the opposition many biblical heroes faced, especially Moses. Moses was God's chosen leader to lead the children of Israel to the Promised Land. But before that time, Moses faced his share of enemies.

From the time of his birth, Moses' life was in danger. Though the Israelites were in slavery in Egypt and were driven to hard labor, they multiplied and were fruitful. This angered the Egyptians so much that Pharaoh instructed the Hebrew midwives to kill all the male babies as soon as they were born.

But God's provision spared Moses' life. His mother hid him for three months and then put him in a basket and floated him on the river, where his sister, Miriam, watched over him. Then Pharaoh's daughter found the baby Moses, adopted him, and brought him up as a well-educated and cultured Egyptian. Only God knew Moses' destiny.

As he lived his ordinary life, Neo had no idea who he was or what his true purpose was. Morphis, which to me represented the Holy Spirit, came to remind him of his identity because Morphis knew all along who Neo was and believed he would become his original self, or as Morphis would say, "You are the one."

I can identify with Moses. Even before my birth, there were forces at work to take my life. My parents, like most young people, mistook their immature infatuation for love. They had plans for their respected futures and certainly having a child at that time was not one of them. My mother was in school and had chosen a career. My father was working at one of the three major car companies in Detroit, making just as much money as his parents. He and my mother were high on life and all that it had to offer, but a child wasn't part of their immediate plans.

One rainy Friday night, my parents were on a date, and my father decided to stop at the famous Hudson Building in downtown Detroit. He wanted to buy an umbrella to keep them from the rain. My mother was a bit more quiet than usual and was slightly nervous, but she finally got up enough nerve to tell my father that she was pregnant. She also told him that three of her friends were pregnant, too. One had already had a "back-alley abortion," and another friend was going to have the procedure done the next day. My mother then said that she was considering having an abortion, too. Along with the dropping of the rain that led my parent into the store to get cover, my mother now has dropped the heavier news to my father, I'm sure he considered the other umbrella (condom) or the lack thereof. With both the news and ultimatums my father emphatically told my mother no and that they would be keeping me and would just have to get married.

Good, Bad, Ugly

One of my all-time favorite rap artists, is gospel rap artist, Lecrae, wrote a song called "Good, Bad, Ugly" about his relationship with a former girlfriend who became pregnant. After hearing a heartbeat that wasn't his or hers, he realized that "the miracle of life had started inside." He laments being selfish and being concerned for only himself. In the song, he admits to taking his girlfriend to the abortion clinic, which was the "day a part of us died."[1]

When most people decide on abortion, they usually think of themselves and what the baby's birth will do to their lives and to their reputations. They may say, "I need to finish school." "This is not the right time in my career." "What will my friends or church members say about me?" "I am too young. I don't have the money for a baby." "I love you, honey, but I am not ready to be a parent at this time." "God is coming back soon, and I don't want to raise a child in these times."

Tonya M. Thomas

While people offer such excuses, they never think to make excuses to put off the sexual act that gave the baby life. If only they had been more conscientious of their time, money, career, and God's coming back when they were slaves to their lusts, then they wouldn't be faced with such a monumental decision in the future. But now that life is present, what would happen if they applied all of their energy and time to successfully bring that life into world?

But despite the enemy's best efforts, I am here. Despite my parents' mistakes, I am here. You are here. We might not have been planned, but in God's divine timing, we are here. When I think of the decision my parents could have made on that rainy night in Detroit, I think of God's ultimate purpose and plan for my life.

Being born out of due time is not about chronological time. Instead, it is *karros*, or God's purpose time. *Karros*, then, is simply where destiny and purpose meet. Though my parents have their role in my life, God's plan and purpose for me is so much bigger than the two of them alone. God allowed my father and my mother to come together in the way they did and in His perfect timing, all to make sure that I arrived here according to plan.

No matter what the circumstances of our births, we are not accidents. Like screenplay writers sometimes start their stories at the end and make the beginning fit that desired end, God in His providential wisdom and knowledge, writes the stories of our lives. I was already predestined and my destiny already planned before time began for such a time as this. Everything that has happened to me up to this point in my journey is leading me to the place God has predestined for me.

Love Is Truth, and Truth Is Love

One of my universal mothers, Ann Marie Wilson, often says, "Love is not 'telt,' but love is felt." In other words, love is not just in telling someone you love that person. Instead, love is in how you make that person feel.

So when people say "I love you," weigh out that statement first and think about how that person makes you feel. Many people are guilty of using the word love so casually, but there's a difference in tossing around "I love you" as an off-the-cuff remark and truly loving someone.

John 3:16 says, "God so loved the world, that he *gave* his only begotten Son" (italics added). True love is always sacrificial in its nature. Our Heavenly Father loves us so much that He gave us something to prove that love. He sacrificed something so dear and precious, the only Son He had.

I am leery of people who can only receive in a relationship. There is absolutely no reciprocity of any sort on their part. That is a relationship that is cursed, not one of love. If you are in any relationship in which you are always the giver or if you are one who is always the receiver, that relationship will yield unhealthy fruit that tends to death, not life. Watch for some of the following signs.

Tonya M. Thomas

People often say they love you so they can get what they want. A man doesn't mind telling a woman sweet things until he can get her into bed. A woman will tell a man how strong and intelligent he is and how he is her hero until his money and influence disappears.

Parents will say they love their children but create a dysfunctional environment for them, especially when the parents themselves are lacking what they feel they are entitled to have. Often, they place their children in inappropriate roles, forcing them to be sounding boards for their bad decisions, making them take on the jobs the absent parent failed to do, manipulating them to choose sides between their parents, and causing their children to constantly work for their approval and love.

Supervisors say they care about their employees and will increase their pay and influence but only if they are in total agreement with their agenda, regardless of how morally sound it is. Although the employees may struggle with this spiritually and emotionally and look for feasible ways to escape, the supervisors convince them of their love and their need to help them through their commitment to their agenda.

So watch out for those who say they love you but don't put actions with their words. When you find the truth, you will find love. The greatest example is found in your relationship with God. God is love, but He is also truth, and where you find one, you will always find the other.

Am I Your Enemy Because I Tell You The Truth?

*If you don't have a dream to develop,
others will use you to develop their dreams.
--Dr. Vekafaswarup Tiriveedhi*

Be careful who you share your dreams with because some people are would-be dream assassinators. Just because they're family members doesn't mean they won't shoot down your dreams. They may have gray hair and hold a position of power in the family or in your church, but that doesn't mean they're wise and will encourage you to reach your full potential.

Don't take it personally. It's not really about you. Some dream-killers are acting out of their own lack, insecurities, and hang-ups. They were never allowed to dream and make strides toward their goals, so it's their nature to try to kill the dreams of others. So when they attempt to kill your dreams and crush your spirit, it's more about the projection of their own disappointing reality than it is about your future. Your future is bright if you want it to be!

You must face/faith forward to your greatest and bright future your…..destiny.

But Jesus said to him, "No one, having put his hand to the plow, and looking back, is fit for the kingdom of God." Luke 9:62

May I just add that a plowman looking back cuts a crooked furrow. Stop looking back that you truly can straighten up and walk and move forward

Tonya M. Thomas

So before you take the words of the dream-killers as truth, think about it. People are the sum total of their experiences. But with dream-killers, when you try to hang your hat on their experiences, you'll always end up with a deficit. Where are their dreams that came true? Where are their successes? What fruit have they produced? What credentials do they have that make them reliable enough to tell you what you should or shouldn't do when they themselves haven't even figured it out yet? If you come up empty on every answer, don't take their advice. Instead, run!

My paternal grandmother was the dream-assassinator for so many people in my family. Fortunately, I was just able to escape, not because I was so strong but because I had taken a strong dose of truth through my heavenly Father.

My grandmother had so many disappointments in her own life that she had decided it was best not to desire anything and always keep her expectations low. This mindset would be the inheritance she left for her children.

My father was my grandmother's firstborn, and it seems he inherited the lion's share of her negativity. This negative mindset for themselves, coupled with their poisonous words for others, gave them great power to cripple and stop the dreams of many in our family.

Aunt Janice, my grandmother's youngest daughter, who is beautiful and creative, wanted to start her own caregiving business. My aunt called me excited about her plans. When people tell me of their hopes and dreams, I am eager to cheer them on. So I was

Am I Your Enemy Because I Tell You The Truth?

excited and pleased that my aunt wanted to share her plans with me and include me in getting her business started. But what made me anxious is what preceded my conversation with her.

During a long season led by God, I would have prayer fellowships. These prayer meetings were the most awesome, liberating, and unified love on display, including breaking of bread (God's Word) with *rhema* (Spirit-inspired) and *logos* (Word). I could have never begun this without the unction of the Holy Spirit and God's Word. I am convinced that the more you get into God's Word, the more God calls you and traps you into the web of great destiny for your secured and ordained purposeful future.

There's no way you can get entangled with God and not have a love for His people and anything good. You develop a desire to share with any and every one, regardless of race, color, religion, creed, sexual orientation, or gender; and you are not limited to any location. Wherever you are, you can be a carrier of the truth and bring that light. People are then attracted to that truth and light and gravitate toward you.

Thankfully, I live in a country where I can pick up my world-changer instrument, the Bible, and read it anytime. So I began to evolve, and my appetite for many things that were temporal changed into fulfilling things that were eternal.

My son, Calvin, and I developed a strong disciplined life of fasting, prayer, and reading and sharing God's Word; and we entered spiritual dimensions untold and almost unlawful to share. The central location for our prayer fellowships was our living room, and that room became "the location of transformation," the portal for us and for many others as well. I became engrafted in God's Word and began to see visions. I wanted to share all of these great and wonderful things with others because these experiences were just too good, just too enormous, not to share and help other people experience them, too.

On one particular occasion, I had a vision that I needed to invite others to come to our home and share in what God was doing for my son and me. I wanted them to partake in His presence and bask in His glory. With great excitement, I invited everyone and anyone to come. I talked to people I knew and strangers I did not know. With each person I reached out to, I was led by the Spirit of God to invite.

Before long, Calvin and other prayer partners began the journey of prayer fellowships in our home. Through this divine source, many people who came not only experienced God's touch of healing, love, restoration, peace, joy, gladness, and fulfilled promises, they also felt His warm embrace shared through others and through His Word.

The lives of those who gathered in my living room were changed forever. Purposes were rediscovered because for many what happened in our fellowships was a confirmation of their personal experiences, while others were introduced to the "new (original) them," and they found true self-discovery.

The same miraculous blessings happened to Aunt Janice. She experienced true self-discovery through the prayer fellowship. I

Am I Your Enemy Because I Tell You The Truth?

invited her to come on several occasions, but when she finally accepted my invitation, I was thrilled.

Aunt Janice arrived early to help me set up, which allowed her to use her talent for preparation and decorating. She can make any room become a heavenly place, and she can turn a fruit and vegetable tray into an elegant affair that would make the queen of England jealous. What's so profound about her gift is that she seems to do it so effortlessly. If it were me, I would put together a snack tray that would look like something a child might have prepared––maybe not even that good. I've learned to stay in my lane and get out of the way and to appreciate the gifts and talents God has given His children.

After consulting God about having the prayer fellowship, we would fast and pray in preparation. Then we would begin the fellowship with praise and worship. Along with music, there was professing, confessing, and declaring the goodness of God, as James 5:13 says: "Is any merry? Let him sing psalms." God's Spirit was always manifested in our midst, and we were filled in His presence.

On the same evening that Aunt Janice came, there were other guests expected, too. As prepared as she was, she could have never been prepared for what would happen next. Both my grandmothers came, along with a host of other witnesses for what God appointed as "Janice Day."

I remember particularly my maternal ,grandmother

Tonya M. Thomas

Mrs. Florence McMichael first with receiving the set of flowers that I had for her, received it differently this time, this was not the first time of her receiving flowers from myself and my son Calvin, for two months prior Calvin and I had rented a limousine and went and picked up my Great Grandmother (my grandmother Florence step-mother), my paternal Grandmother Mrs. Jerelstein Hall and lastly my biological mother and treated them to an elegant affair for everyone that was even picked-up Calvin came out looking debonair and handsome with his fine suite and great looks, while the driver would hold the door open Calvin would go to their house door and greet them with a dozen of roses while escorting them to the car. On many accounts would Calvin and I just go and show love to our grandparents without any holiday or birthday but just because.

But for this event my grandmother which would tell me later as to why the look she had was there, she would later share that she experience something in my home and saw in my countenance something she could not describe, other than there was a joy that was unspeakable. She would later share that the flowers literally lasted over 30 days this was such a miraculous event, for roses to ever last that long and yet look and remain fresh.

What I concluded for her that evening, and with Janice was nothing less than a newer and higher level of a great release of God's Glory cloud

Although those who attended got what they were expecting and more, God divinely set up something extra for Aunt Janice. She

Am I Your Enemy Because I Tell You The Truth?

was beautiful and gifted, but her life had been interrupted by the perceptions she had adopted and believed about herself because of certain circumstances and the bad choices she had made. Even worse, she listened to her mother's poisonous words.

That night, we reached great heights in praise and worship, and God brought Aunt Janice up in the Spirit. She was on His divine stage, and He glammed her out with His glam squad of angels and gave her a make-over. He let her know that she was His workmanship, beautifully and wonderfully made. Prophet Karen, who had made her first visit to the fellowship, would be the vessel and conduit for God's great and majestic power toward my aunt.

The word was so fierce and powerful that we looked at Aunt Janice like the children of Israel looked at Moses when he descended the mountain after having been in the presence of God. We almost could not handle the light that was upon her. Prophetically, resurrection, life, and truth were spoken to her as the tears streamed down her face. She was reborn and transformed to her original self.

The prophet spoke peace, joy, deliverance, and more into my aunt's life that night. When God speaks, He speaks clearly. With pinpoint accuracy, he spoke through Prophet Karen the precise details and every intricate part that was heard, and those words served as notice to all of us and declared God's voice into the atmosphere.

Tonya M. Thomas

Like midwives, those of us gathered at the fellowship rejoiced with sheer joy at Aunt Janice's breakthrough. We were humbled and honored that our Father allowed us to partake and witness His majesty and good will in her life. This breakthrough was sealed.

But not only did she have us witness her breakthrough, along with those in the heavenly realm, but the enemy of her faith likewise witnessed and was not at all pleased. The enemy came in like a flood, and although the Spirit of the Lord was ready to lift

Am I Your Enemy Because I Tell You The Truth?

up a standard against him, my aunt did not have her battle clothes on nor did she feed her faith at that time, so she was vulnerable to his attack.

Later, trials would arise for my aunt. Trials are not unusual for mature believers. They know the enemy has a perfect hatred toward anyone who is walking in truth. Just as a side-note if ever you doubt your salvation, let me tell you the mere fact you are going through is a tell-tale sign, for remember if you were his he wouldn't attack you but know that you are going through and will eventually end up in your promise land.

Being the cowardly and wicked character he is, he always hits below the belt. He's done his homework on you and has studied all of your weaknesses, vulnerabilities, and proclivities. He has a PHD. On your weakness and has a Masters on your demise. His plan is that he can hit you where it hurts most and knock you out of God's will, causing you to miss your divine purpose, destiny, and blessings.

After Janice experience this awakening she would go on her way of preparations. This involved her now in spending more time and investing in herself rather than my grandmother. You see up unto this point my grandmother literally became a benefactor of my Aunt Janice dysfunctions or her lacks thereof. Some people would never want to see you free because after all, your freedom would take something away from them. This is no difference in Pharaoh letting the children of Israel go, to a pimp telling a prostitute "how much he needs her", to a person just learning how to drive and learning the directions of a city as oppose to relying on jitney, cab, or Uber. The conclusion of all them is that all have been given an opportunity to make money/time or simply advance their agendas for the help of you, so to have you free will inevitably take something from them. So they will always oppose your freedom and will fight anyone who will assist you in your breakout. People will always capitalize on your lacks and ignorance. Though my grandmother often assist Janice it came with a grave price, and the attempt of her having to come back to her rather helping to become self-sufficient. "Give a person a fish he will eat for the day, teach him how to fish he will eat for a lifetime".

Well Janice was on her way and making great strides first internally and later externally as I had assisted her with resources and the more emotional support she had flown to heights unknown. Then the unthinkable occurred, she had called me, I almost did not recognize her voice because she was crying so bad, I immediately go into protective mode and ready to fight whoever done it. She ask me to come to get her and I did, she came out the house, because she was staying with my grandmother. When I arrived to pick her up, like an abused child she came out of a secured place to immediately leave with me. As we would drive she poured out tears like a running faucet, all while trying to catch her breath in between.

A true massacre had taken place, my grandmother, her mother used her tongue as a lethal injection and stripped her of all she had believed, desired, dreamed.

Am I Your Enemy Because I Tell You The Truth?

Simply because of the dynamic of their relationship was my grandmother as successful as I tried as much as possible to pick-her up the true-enemy of her soul, had sent in troops of word assassination "you a fool to believe you could do anything, you are not smart enough, you aint got know business to even think you can do better" and through my grandmother they were successful, she began to sound like a scene from the movie Color Purple with Harpo talking to Ms. Ceeley "you aint got nothing, you ugly, and you aint even a good of a cook, (though he ate off her life all that time". When you are losing yourself from your captures they will flip the script and tell you what you are not, which is always fascinating because when they have you there no complaints and if you were not all of that then why are they messing with you?

You see it is true "when the unclean spirit goes out of a man, he come back taking with himself seven other spirits more wicked then himself and the last state of that person is worse than the first Matthew "12"43-45. That verse goes unto say that the evil spirit finds that soul empty, swept, and garnished, it is must that when we get liberated that we fill up the place for which we got clean, filling that space with first God's word and praise and worship. It is also imperative that you change your environment and people in your life, regardless of who they are, you must remember your life depends on it, and you are worth it.

Tonya M. Thomas

Anger Brings Damage and Loss

The Bible says, "Anger rests in the bosom of fools." Anger is an intense emotion and is one letter away from danger. Often, though, we focus more on anger's visible effects instead of its root causes.

Some people shrug off the anger of others, calling it silly or ignorant. But perhaps they don't take anger seriously because they don't understand where it comes from and why it affects people as it does.

I recall a time where some of my behavior that was recognized and later shared among extended family about my ability to fight because of the stories that proceeded it, the thought was I enjoyed or found some pleasure in fighting. That could not have been further from the truth. I am the eldest and because of the dynamics in our home my sibling often came to me in assurance for refuge and safety and knew they will always have it, regardless of what served as the threat. There was a time when my younger sister came home in such a panic and sheer fear about a gang of girls that tried to fight her. When she came through the door both my parents were in her view and with their attempt to bring some resolve she ran pass them screaming for me. I immediately came to her and off we go out of the house. I immediately learned where the leader lived and went to her home and settled our affairs. I fought even then with the strategic of getting the leader to not having to continue some ongoing anything.

The major problem with that was that my sister who was than bullied; after my success of the fight and my having her to come

Am I Your Enemy Because I Tell You The Truth?

over and get a few hits in as well, because I did not believe the success was done until I showed her to confront and never be scared of anything and anyone again, would later back fire. As truth would have it, all the neighborhood took the news both to the school and surrounding that my sister Tina bough into the hype of the praises of winning the fight and liked it so much that she later became a weak bully herself.

Many times, angry people also have trouble communicating, so they are often misunderstood and ignored. Communication can mean life or death in many situations. The lack of communication builds barriers and allows anger to fester and get out of control. As human beings, we just want our voices to be heard and understood, and when that doesn't happen, it can fuel our anger. It is a must that you confront what ails you. As an African American I can tell you, our culture has been notoriously known for not dealing with matters properly and thereby lending unhealthy results.

Many of us was raised to believe that "what goes on in this house stays in this house". We don't always embrace the need of confronting all issues regardless of its shame in a healthy way, counseling is necessary, releasing the pain is ultimately bringing that act/shame/issue/regret/ to the forefront of the light of truth. Otherwise anything that remains in the dark/secret/stronghold will become the death of that person and their relationships, job opportunities, and many advancements. Unresolved issues are often the fruit of the root of displaced anger. You need to place anger in the light of truth that it can lose its strongholds on your life and set you free from its constraints and all its ill will. So you cuss your mate out for a very insignificant thing, you say inconceivable words to your children from a pain that has fester from your childhood, you lead your fellow- staff with a hard iron fist simply because you were abused earlier in life and have everyone paying for it, worst still you now have an appointed authority in life such as a police officer and because you were bullied and mistreated as a child from your peers and others; now everyone that is stopped is subject to your wrath not the law. Please know that not dealing with something is dealing with something. Why hold onto what's killing you inside.

Do not Fret because of evildoers, Nor be envious of the workers of iniquity, For they shall soon be cut down the grass, and wither as the green herb. Psalm 37:1-2

Humility is the ultimate key, you have to learn and practice what I call the 1-2 punch "Relax! Don't React!", I have learned that this two hitter knock-out always wins the fight. You don't have to ever entertain the foolish. Your responding and displaying meekness, which is ultimately anger in control set you up to win every time.

Real Communication Reveals Truth

A defense attorney told me about a case she was working on. The case involved a man who had gone to a bar with friends. He didn't speak English very well, and in the course of the night, he and his friends got into a fight.

During the fight, his friends left him at the bar alone. He was drunk and injured and needed help. He called 911, but the operator had a difficult time understanding him, so she was unable to send help. The man was bleeding profusely and later died from his injuries.

When I heard this story, my heart broke. I thought about the language barrier that prevented this man from getting the medical help he needed. It made me think about how communication barriers keep us from getting the healing and help we need as well. When we're angry and we're not able to communicate with our family members, spouses, children, or co-workers, we create more chaos in our lives and in theirs, too.

While working for the state of Michigan, I handled unapproved claims for the unemployed. I was the youngest African American woman in the department. At first, I was excited to work with people twice my age. I enjoyed having the opportunity to receive the wealth of knowledge and experience that they had to offer.

But then everything changed. During my first week on the job, I discovered that my "seasoned" co-workers sat in the break room and ridiculed our clients. Many of the claims that we received were initially rejected because of misspelled words or illegible writing. Some of our clients had little education but were doing the best they could to fill out the paperwork required by the state. But instead of helping them fill out the forms correctly so the paperwork would be accepted, my callous co-workers laughed at our clients and made fun of their poorly worded forms.

Tonya M. Thomas

I was so disappointed. While I don't believe in enabling people to stay where they are, I do believe in helping people to do better if they can. Instead of helping our clients fix the simple written mistakes, which would have made their claims acceptable in the short-term and helped our clients get the help they needed in the long-term, my co-workers decided that it was easier just to laugh at them for sport. Unfortunately, in the case of our clients, it was another example of people not being able to communicate and get the help they needed.

Today, people say they're just "keepin' it real," but that's misguided thinking. "Keepin' it real" can keep you broke, it can keep you down, and it can keep you stuck in a place you don't need to be. Some people are more skilled, more competent, and more intelligent than others, but they have a bad attitude, so they don't get far. Communication and a humble, grateful, gracious, and kind attitude can make all the difference in a person being hired or another being fired. I have been given positions much quicker than I expected, not because I was more qualified but because I had the right attitude.

When you decide that you're only going do the bare minimum to get by or certain things are not in your job description, then you've set yourself up to be in a position to be left behind. Going the extra yard, especially when it's not asked for or expected shows that you are a person of great character and integrity.

Perhaps you believe that good looks, being in on the latest gossip, or playing office politics will help you climb the career ladder.

Am I Your Enemy Because I Tell You The Truth?

While those things might advance you so far, you will always have to look over your shoulder for the person coming up behind you because of how you got where you are. Instead, work hard, and be a person of integrity. Don't do just enough to get by, and go over and beyond what's expected of you. In that way, you open up more opportunities to come your way.

Don't Live Under their Radar
In this life, there will always be people who resent your progress. They don't believe they can achieve what you have achieved, so they will put obstacles in your way or work to drag you down where they are. You will meet such people at work, in your family, and in other relationships, even in places of worship but you can't let them hold you back. You can't let anyone or anything keep you from becoming who God intended you to be and living in liberty. Your true self bears a light that is so exhilarating that it cannot be denied by anyone who comes into your presence. It demands a level of attention that cannot be overlooked or underestimated. When you come into contact with the true you, your authentic you,
   It is exciting. You almost cannot contain yourself!
   It's like when a person is presented with a beautifully wrapped gift. Although the person might want to rip open the package to find out what's inside, it's difficult to mess up such pretty wrapping paper. The person will usually take time to admire the beautiful wrapping and then carefully undo the tape and ribbons so as not to ruin the paper. The person also is aware that despite the value

of the gift inside, the intricate wrapping indicates that someone went to great care and paid a lot of attention to detail in wrapping the present.

It's interesting that some people who may not have much respect for their own things tend to respect others and their things, especially things that are shiny, new, and clean. I've seen people park next to a clean, shiny car, and I noticed that they took great care when opening their doors so as not to scratch the clean car. Although they didn't know anything about the owner of the clean car, because of the appearance of the car, and how well it has been taken care of they treated it with great respect.

People treat one another the same way. They don't have to know anything about you, but when in your presence, they might see something that causes them to give you the utmost respect. That's why it's important to be a person of integrity and character at all times. You never know whose watching you and inspecting the "wrapping" you present to the world. If they can get a glimpse of the true you by just observing the light they see in your presence, they will want to know more.

Your challenge, though, comes in understanding your identity and embracing your purpose for being here at this time and in this space. It would be a total tragedy if when you die all you have is the space between your birth and your death filled with nothing but confusion, regrets, and fear leaving you with just that weighty dash between the dates. Here's a healthy dose of truth: You just wasted time. Remember, you can always replace, cars, homes, girlfriends, boyfriends, friends, and jobs, but you can never replace time. Time is the most valuable possession you own and is given equally to all.

Generational Grace

It's not the material things you leave for your children that are of great value; it's what you leave in them, those intangible things that you spent a lifetime sowing into their spirits so that they can one day reap a harvest of that is of far greater value than money or possessions.

Leave them a legacy of hope and the encouragement that they can venture outside of where they are and live a good life, moving forward into their destiny. Don't be a dream-killer or one who sows into them only negative words and curses. Instead, give them what they'll need in life long after you're gone.

I honor both my great-grandmothers. The stories I've heard about them gives me more insight into my own life's journey, but generational, my family has been filled with dysfunction, much of which has trickled down to me, and I'm yet recovering from it. A person's greatest enemies come from within, and many of my family members aren't fighting an external enemy that tries to keep them down. Instead, they are fighting themselves and the bad choices they have made.

Sometimes it's easier to fight external enemies. Many times, they're easier to spot, and you can size them up and determine just how best to fight them. However, it's more difficult to fight the enemies within (enemy-in-a-me). The internal enemies we face are intangible but cause great damage. For example, fear, negativity, depression, low self-esteem, insecurity, and narrow-mindedness are just some of the internal enemies we find ourselves fighting. We may brag about telling off a co-worker or swinging our fist at a jerk at the club, but we remain defeated by our internal enemies.

And the people who bring out the worst in us are sometimes as close to us as we are to ourselves: our families. My father and his mother have played their part in our family's dysfunction by controlling the lives of so many of us in a negative way. Unfortunately, they relish playing such destructive roles and have enjoyed seeing certain family members suffer. You would think that a person gets wiser as he or she grows older, but when it comes to my grandmother, all I can say is that some people grow old while others grow up.

I love my family, and they aren't without their good qualities. But many of the characteristics that have been passed from one generation to the other weren't in any way good or healthy. In fact, many of these qualities have reared their heads over and over again as generational curses. You see sometimes the challenges you are yet trying to best understand let along get a grasps on came to you without your personal involvement, you simply inherited some dysfunctional proclivities.

Like going to the doctor where he can better prognosis your needs he inquires about certain medical history of your family to better understand you. You may want to do the same, ask yourself besides having daddy's long arms, and momma's high cheek

Am I Your Enemy Because I Tell You The Truth?

bones. What is this verbal abuse you carry like a ready-rifle, great granddaddy did not like to work or marry, what about silent treatment you give your mate because like your father he didn't speak, what about the proclivities of always falling into excessiveness of working too much, three generations of drug abuse and poverty, can't stay with one woman, having children by several different men, jealous of your sister and sleeping with her mates; only to later learn that grandmother did the same thing with her sister, coincidence..........I think not.

Every family is different. Over time, they develop certain values and beliefs. Those family elders have great influence and often shape how those who come after them live their lives. However, that influence or power can be used for good or for evil. Unfortunately, some family elders use their power to control and manipulate their children and grandchildren, leaving a legacy of poisonous words, hatred, and narrow-minded thinking.

So you might find that there will come a time when you will simply have to walk away from all the drama and chaos. You will have to walk away from family members, or anyone else, who are toxic and do nothing but drag you down. Instead, surround yourself with people who make you laugh and help you forget the bad and focus on the good. Love the people who treat you right, and pray for the ones who don't.

While we shouldn't live in our pasts, we should study the lessons from the past and glean from them those things that will help us in our future. We can also learn from the lessons of others so that we don't repeat their mistakes, wasting valuable time and energy spinning our wheels.

In order for *his*tory or *her*story to be told, it has to be well-communicated with a level of understanding for the hearers. What often happens is that while the elders in our families are teaching life lessons and telling their stories, they are ultimately reproducing their own kind––functional or dysfunctional. But we can't become stuck in their mistakes. We have to ask questions, and sometimes we have to challenge traditional thinking. We don't have to just accept what's handed down to us because that's the way it's always been done.

Stop and ask, Why are we doing this? How is this way of doing things helping us move forward? If we continue to do things this way, are we better or worse off than we were before? How can we do things better?

For by thy words thou shalt be justified; and by thy words thou shalt be justified, and by thy words thou shalt be condemned.
––Matthew 12:37

I once heard a story about a man who questioned his wife on how she cooked the ham for Sunday dinner. He had noticed that whenever she cooked ham, his wife cut pieces off both ends of it before placing it in the roasting pan.

"Honey, why do you always cut the ham that way?"

"I don't know. But that's how my mama taught me to do it, and I've been cooking it that way ever since."

Am I Your Enemy Because I Tell You The Truth?

Out of curiosity, the man called his mother-in-law and asked her about the odd cuts on the ham.

"When you cook ham, why do you always cut pieces off the ends?" he asked.

Puzzled, his mother-in-law said, "I really don't know. That's just the way my mother told me to do. All I know is that it tastes good to me. Don't you like the way my daughter cooks it?"

"Of course! It tastes fine, but I just wanted to know why you taught my wife to cut pieces off the ends of the ham. I guess I'll have to call Big Mama. Maybe she'll know the answer."

Big Mama, though 93 and deaf in one ear, was still sharp as a tack. Although she had some trouble at first hearing the man's question, she finally understood what he was asking.

"Why do I cut the ends off the ham? Well, baby, when I first got married, all I had was a small pan, and the ham was too big to fit in it. So, I would cut pieces off both ends of the ham so it would fit into the pan!"

After talking to Big Mama, the man thought about all the ham his mother-in-law and his wife had wasted over the years. He told the story to his wife, who was just as shocked as he was at the answer.

"My mother and I thought we were cutting the ham just to enhance the taste. But I'm gonna keep on cutting the ends of the ham when I cook it because if it ain't broke, there's no need to fix it!"

The man laughed at his wife's stubbornness as he walked away and said, "No, it ain't broke, just wasted."

Tonya M. Thomas

The good news is that the truth begins with you. So despite the negativity of your family culture, God can still use all of that for your good and replace the enemy's lies with truth. God's plans for you are good and are unchanging. He can take that same dysfunctional family situation and use it to propel you into your destiny. So don't lose hope because you came from less-than-ideal circumstances. Maybe you are the chosen, individual to help break the chains and set your family free. Never get discourage because some changes may not immediately bear its fruits. Like a seed underground it is always working, though you may not see it above ground, just be patient and know if you have assisted 1 family member or more importantly yourself and your household, you already have the victory There is still hope with you. There is no need to waste anymore ham/life.

CHAPTER 2
From Victim to Victor

*If you are willing to embrace truth,
you will forever remain a victor.*

Victim

Going from victim to victor is often easier said than done, but with God's help, it is possible. I can say this because I did it.

I grew up in a dysfunctional family and experienced things no child should ever have to. The most challenging experience was having my virginity taken from me through molestation, by a close relative. What made it worse was that the adults in my life dismissed my pain and tried to bury it, but that only produced shame, embarrassment, fear, and rage in me. I felt isolated, despised, and rejected. My life as I knew it had been shattered, and no one seemed to care.

But the little girl in me continued to cry out. She always had a voice, but no one wanted to listen. They robbed her of that voice. Even today, she screams and at times will come out unexpectedly and at the slightest provocation. No one protected her and made her feel safe, so her pain drove me to want to protect others. Although I had to always silence the pain inside, I decided I would be everyone else's hero.

Tonya M. Thomas

As a child, when I would fight for myself or for others, I would become so enraged that it was as if I had blacked out and became The Incredible Hulk. I was someone else. The person I was fighting became all the people who had failed me: my parents, the person who molested me, other adults who failed to protect me. After the fights, I sometimes felt sorry for the person I had beaten up because the damage was so severe.

Looking back, I was most angry because my parents weren't parental at all. They were never nurturing, protective, or reliable—all of the things children need from their parents. My parents failed on all counts.

What hurt even more was that they could be loving and kind to everyone else, including other people's children, but not to my siblings and me. In fact, my brother Taurus and I would laugh when we heard our cousins or neighbors talk about how great our parents were. We said to each other, "Who in the world are they talking about? Surely, they can't be talking about our parents!" If they only knew what our parents were really like, they wouldn't think they were so great after all.

It wasn't as if my siblings and I didn't try to earn our parents love. We did everything we thought they wanted, but it never happened. But while my childhood was less than idyllic, my story wasn't over.

I did not then nor now believed that, that was going to be my plight or my siblings, I did become this strong mother hen over their lives. I would become what I believed and wanted to see. I began with my siblings I prepared our home like combination of

Am I Your Enemy Because I Tell You The Truth?

the "Brady's and the Cosby's", I would cook for us prepare, have us spend quality time with each other, and always have my significant others take strong interest in my siblings.

Even the more I wanted them to always realize that they had a voice and they were very important I told them and demonstrated to them how loved they were and how great they were. I would even have us have regular "family-talks", where they voice all of their concerns and appreciations, I recall my brother Taurus telling me "you the one who told us to forgive that "Nigga", he was talking about my father.

The reality is I like all children even though our parents were and can be dysfunctional the child in all of us longs for that wholeness of the parent. As children we will have the patience of job to see the manifestations of the parent would long to see from our parents with all of their potential. In hope regardless if the parent was a workaholic, jobless, homeless, drug abuser, in jail, left the family, moved away; regardless of that parent indiscretions there is a hole in every child heart that fits their parent's figure that they longed to have filled.

You might have been the victim of abandonment from family, marriage, social club, even your place of worship, but when you connect with the "Truth" who is Jesus because He's the way you will come from victim to victor.

Tonya M. Thomas

Victor

Just because your life started out in less-than-perfect conditions doesn't mean you have to give up. Maybe you had a great childhood, but you've gone through difficult circumstances as an adult that have left you broken, depressed, and discouraged. God still loves you and has a plan for your life. It's not over!

Don't let anyone tell you that this is all there is, that you can't do better and don't deserve better. You can leave victimhood behind, and you can be a victor. Your story doesn't have to end with poverty, divorce, bankruptcy, abandonment, or death of a loved one. God writes your story, and He's already proclaimed that through Him you're more than a conqueror!

My childhood was marred by neglect, molestation, and abuse, but God made me an overcomer. According to most statistics, I should have been on drugs, landed in jail, became promiscuous, became a violator, practiced homosexuality, ended up dead. But statistics don't direct my destiny. My heavenly Father does, and He says that I'm a winner!

Despite the pain of my circumstances, I became self-reliant, responsible, relentless, and victorious; and I know if I can survive and thrive given my past, you can, too. My past didn't define my destiny, and neither does yours. You can go from being a victim to being a victor because in Christ, you are more than a conqueror! You are God's chosen warrior. Look at what you have already overcame. You my friend are truly amazing and you have shown

Am I Your Enemy Because I Tell You The Truth?

to possess some incredible strengths to have endured what you have had no other choice to endure. I applaud you my warrior>

Warrior Defined

We talk about the warrior spirit, but seldom do we define what that means. A warrior is someone who faces conflict.

A warrior's body may be the weapon, but how that weapon is used depends on the heart and mind of the warrior, the spirit. Warriors move toward a quick and strategic conclusion to confront, not away from it. They know avoidance only postpones the inevitable and never resolves conflict and holds a single, concentrated focus on the objective, the mission, or the goal. They know that fear comes from negative fantasies about the future. By staying focused on the present task at hand, there is no fear.

Warriors accept that death is inevitable and while not wanting to die, they are not afraid to die. They save lives, even if it means taking some, and believe in a deep code of honor. They welcome responsibility and accountability and make and take no excuses.

A disciplined life is the norm for warriors, and they know there are no shortcuts. They see every challenge as another opportunity to practice and improve their skills. They make others uncomfortable ourselves. We are to live in such a way that other people see something different about us. We are called Christians because we are supposed to be Christ-like, or like Christ, so we must make every effort to think, act, and live like we know Him.

Even the heathen knows when we are authentic. The Bible says, "By their fruits ye shall know them" (Matthew 7:20). If you're not bearing any fruit, or you're bearing the wrong kind of fruit, check your spirit, and then check in with the Holy Spirit.

The Awakening

The transformation from victim to victor is an awesome experience on so many levels. When you make such a transition, you are now empowered for a life that is filled with amazing possibilities. Through Christ, there is nothing you can't do.

For a great example, read the story of David and Goliath (1 Samuel 17). In that battle, David was the underdog. Even men bigger, stronger, and older than he was were afraid of the Philistine giant.

King Saul offered young David his royal armor, but David knew he wouldn't win the fight with someone else's shield, helmet, and sword. Instead, David drew on his experience as a shepherd and the many close encounters he had had with bears and lions. He told Saul, "The Lord that delivered me out of the paw of the lion, and out of the paw of the bear, he will deliver me out of the hand of [Goliath]" (1 Samuel 17:37).

So, David took five smooth stones and his slingshot and went out to face Goliath. Despite being doubted by King Saul and his army, David killed the giant with one stone.

You and I face our own giants. Some of them are physical ones that we can see, while others are not so easily seen. We fight

Am I Your Enemy Because I Tell You The Truth?

external as well as internal enemies, and many times we leave the fight defeated and broken. But this is where we need to follow David's example. Take the five stones (T.R.U.T.H) just as David did. Go after any Goliath that raises its head to threaten you, and hit it in the head.

To the soul, truth is refreshing, totally thirst-quenching, and amazingly satisfying. When you experience pure truth, there's nothing like it. You will find yourself able to defeat those old enemies of the mind and of the heart. John 8:32 says, "And ye shall know truth, and the truth shall make you free." When you can walk in the liberty of the truth, you can leave victimhood and become a victor in Christ, but the power lies in your knowing the truth.

Many of us have lived our lives surrounded by lies and deceit, so when we hear truth, it's often painful and unpleasant. We might even do whatever we can to run from it or avoid it. But like most medical procedures that might be painful at first, there is often the end result, which is relief and freedom from pain.

The surgery of truth removes the layers of deceit. God is the Truth Specialist, and His Word is part of the remedy. It might feel as if you're undergoing surgery without anesthesia, but it's necessary to remove years of pain so you can experience the healing that only truth can bring.

You may have to learned that first you could have been sincerely wrong, in error, and have desperate need of being healed. Sometimes, lies for the moment appear to be more palatable and pleasant to the ear. But lies are the devil's territory and an abomination to

Tonya M. Thomas

God. In fact, the Bible tells us that the devil is the father of lies. Lying will inevitably assassinate your character and destroy your integrity

Lies destroy relationships, families, business, and places of worship, companies, and lives. Nothing is immune to the power of lies. Imagine you spent all of your life believing that the man who raised you, gave you his last name, and said he was your father really wasn't. Can you imagine the devastation you would feel as you realize your whole life was all a lie? What about sharing your heart and life with someone with plans to spend your future with them only later to learn they were living a double life, you were not their only one. You signed a contract for a musical career while entrusting a manger to whom you thought had your best interest to handle your business affairs. Only later to learn you have a very small return not even a fraction of the aforesaid promise.

Let's say you entrusted your life's savings with a company that promised to make a good return on your investment. The company's representative has promised you that there's no way you can lose your money, although the representative knows the company is about to go bust. The next week, you receive a letter informing you that every penny you've worked so hard to save is gone with no hope of seeing it again. Can you imagine the anguish you would feel because of the company's lies?

Or consider an example a little closer to home. What if your best friend betrayed you? Your friend is someone with whom you've shared your deepest secrets. You've confided in this person, trusted

Am I Your Enemy Because I Tell You The Truth?

this person, and depended on this person to be there for you. But then your best friend cheats with your spouse but continues to lie to you that everything is fine and nothing has changed. How deeply hurt would you be?

In each of these situations, the truth would have been painful, especially in the short-term. But in the long-term, the truth would have been far less painful than the devastation of the lies that were told.

Many people trust in unreliable resources to provide them with truth. They think that unless NBC, CNN, ABC, or TBN say it, they won't believe it. The "powers that be" of this world control the lie and take it to unfounded heights because many people don't ask the real questions. They just accept whatever "facts" they're given and believe what they're told, but to their detriment.

For example, entertainers and athletes appear to be wealthy, and they often show off their beautiful mansions and expensive cars and jewelry, while they jet off on exotic vacations. Some people get so caught up in these displays of wealth that they miss what's really going on.

The public doesn't always see the machinations behind the scenes. We don't see the owners, managers, publicists, staff, and other hangers-on who eat up a large percentage of the money and control what the celebrities can and cannot do. But if we believe what we see on TV, we can feel envy toward celebrities and even toward those closer to home.

Tonya M. Thomas

In other cases, some of those who are rich present another type of image that is deceiving. Publicly, they never reveal just how wealthy, powerful, and influential they are. It's only behind the scenes that you can see what really happens. Money makes things move in this world, and there are some extremely powerful people behind many of the essential resources that regular people like you and I use every day. And the people who control those things control the media, supplies of food and water, and other things that we come in contact with.

So we need to open our eyes and see what's real, not the false reality we've been presented. We can't just believe every lie that come down from the powerful people at the top.

All sorts of lies come from our government or other groups of influential people and are channeled through the media. One year, you'll hear that milk is healthy, only to hear a year later that it is unhealthy.

You might hear that there's no known cure for cancer but then read about research that says, yes, there is possibly a cure. Then you'll hear that all white policemen are racist or all black men are criminals with imagery attached you are led to believe that it is true. I personally have met and embraced white policeman that have treated me like I was their family and I them I think about officer William Waters of Nashville, this impeccable man of integrity had regareded his position with truth and handled it with wisdom and care. On the other hand I have met some very viscious servicemen of the law like attorney Ryan Caldwell of Nashville

Am I Your Enemy Because I Tell You The Truth?

who had deliberately taken his power of the law and have executed his knowledge with intention on hurting people deliberately that he can build his reputation. All while many higher officials are capitalizing on prison and its free labor, its expensive phone calls to the expansion buildings of prison walls rather building learning institutions and employment that is economically fair.

Football the American favorite sport is humanly acceptable and will not have any physical or mental consequences, the war and loosing men is necessary," the powers that be" would not even place their own children in harm's way, but they don't mind if yours are. When your children who was in one piece return home from war from some traumatic experience, they pin a ribbon of honor on their chests, leaving you and your loved ones to pick up their broken pieces.

"The powers that be" will have us all fall into a race war to implant fear and demise one towards another. They will have you convinced all while furthering their agenda that you **need** certain things that just 25 years ago would not even serve any purpose at all. Have you ever stopped and wonder, how our seniors who had less education, less comforts, less accumulation of things, yet they have lived longs lives, build monuments, made great discoveries, raised healthy children. There was never a high crime rate, children did not disrespect their own parents let along the communities. Farmers were able to grow their crops and raise their families, without fear of being "strong armed" by the government to produce unhealthy crops.

Tonya M. Thomas

The new "tether" oh I'm sorry the phone, not only tracks your whereabouts but you pay a hefty fee to be "controlled", in fact the government will tell you let your phone be "smart" let us "CIRI" think for you.

In fact the life as we know is becoming to look and feel like the movie "I Robot" starring the great actor Will Smith. Where the robots (technology has taken over the world) we all have experienced the challenges when there is computer failure of any sort many things completely shut –down.

This coming of total technological society has vastly come. The number system is already in place, the cashless society is already on the rise, everyone and anyone can get a credit card. Like Will Smith character, he sought and saw beyond what appeared to be "convenience" and saw the **control,** once he traced the greater benefactor he solved the case of the lie. Those ought to be the questions that should be asked both by the American people and ultimately the human race **who benefits from our dysfunction** of racial wars, broken families, food illness, medical depravity, and man-made religious laws. Once the lies are removed, you can open your eyes to the truth, which is real power. You begin to understand that those in power always keep themselves out of light, but they are still present there, behind the scenes. There are systematic designs that have been strategically put into place for the good of those who pull the strings.

Am I Your Enemy Because I Tell You The Truth?

There is a group more powerful than any of the wealthiest people you can think of. This is the best plan of a great chess player: to make strategic moves to conquer and to checkmate the opponent.

Racism is by design. The "haves" and the "have-nots" don't operate in the same universe. From their exalted thrones, some of the powerful "haves" control everything in the world of the powerless "have-nots."

I don't have all the answers in life, but I know that what we see now is an escalation of what was. I once toured the Ford mansion in Detroit. The house was filled with the most modern conveniences of early to mid-twentieth century. Where they had microwaves in the 1960's, my family didn't have such a luxury until the 1980's. Just another example of how the "haves" of the world will always have the best of everything in advanced.

Another truth is about the so-called war on drugs. If you think dealers wear gold chains, drive expensive cars, and carry a bundle of money in their pockets, you've been fed a lie. Though some of the main drugs are grown in other countries altogether yet they seem to make it here in our country pass the "govern borders". Most of the street pushers never been out of their cities let along the country. They don't often have valid driver license let along passport .T he biggest drug dealers wear lab coats and have medical degrees. They prescribe medicine unnecessarily in order to make money because they know that their patients will come back time and time again for more. The patients have been convinced that they need their drugs, and will do almost anything to get them.

Tonya M. Thomas

People addicted to prescription medicine are the same as crack heads. We just call them by different names. There are senior citizens who are eating dog food just so they can afford their medication. How is that different from the sexual exchanges crack heads have had just to get their next fix?

We have been taught that there is no cure for cancer or AIDS, but we're encouraged to give to this fundraiser or that charity so a cure can be found. More money is raised for "research," but where does all this money go? After all these years and all the billions of dollars that have been raised, why haven't any cures been discovered, though we can create technology with all of its brilliance?

Whenever the truth is embraced, you will come into the light out of all the darkness and dispel the lies that have had you bamboozled. You will no longer feel the need of compromising to get ahead on the job. You won't sell out your own people for notoriety and fame. You will recognize quickly that the powerful people and their agenda are all lies. They've simply set us up to run this rat race with little cheese as they sit back in their comfortable gated communities with every luxury imaginable. They don't care about the rest of us. They only want to further their agenda while keeping everyone else entangled in the lie.

That's one of the reasons I've written this book. I want to let you know that you and I are on a quest for the truth, and we're not alone. Despite the enemy's lies and attempts to silence us, there are many brave and courageous truth-followers who have stood against

Am I Your Enemy Because I Tell You The Truth?

the system of the lie, including Jesus Christ, his disciples, and the apostle Paul, and David my biblical heroes, who stood against the law of religion, flesh-led practices, and the devil. Contemporary heroes such as Fredrick Douglass, Harriet Tubman, just to name a few, along with:

Martin Luther King brought light to injustice toward all members of the human race. Malcom X exposed the ill practices and deeds of Elijah Muhammad and other Muslims.

Dr. Bennet Omalu, the brilliant forensic neuropathologist, made the first discovery of CTE, a football-related brain trauma, and fought for the truth to be known. Omalu's research put him at odds with the NFL and has caused controversy in the sports world.

Shirley Sherrod is an African American woman who was fired from her position as Georgia State Director of Rural Development for the USDA. She was accused of making racist remarks at a NAACP event. These allegations cost Sherrod her reputation, and the White House called for her resignation. Later, a recording of the event was played, and the full context of her remarks was reviewed. The White House apologized, and she was offered a better position with higher pay, but she refused it.

Sandra Bland came to the consciousness of truth only to do what true light-givers do and that is to share the light of truth with others through social media. This precious jewel of a fine warrior sat in a jail cell for a bond of $5,000, ten percent of which was $500. Yet her family, who was made aware the amount they needed to pay, could not come up with $500 and allowed Bland to sit in jail for three days, making them the greatest culprits in her plight. The number five means grace, and Bland's family didn't show her grace.

Her family, like the families of most of us warriors, did not understand Bland's passion or her divine assignment of rendering the truth. They probably not only embraced it but thought that she was, to some degree, a nuisance and a problem. Perhaps when Bland was arrested by police, they may have even said that she deserved it. That's the only way to explain why they didn't bail her out any sooner. A true and loving family would have acted quickly and with compassion to save a loved one.

There are families who will rescue their loved ones, no matter the costs. There are mothers who have put their houses up for collateral, while others have past-due bills because they couldn't afford to let their loved ones remain in trouble.

The courts awarded Bland's family over a million dollars because of her alleged suicide. And although they couldn't come up with $500 to set her free, they will now get to spend the money that was given for her life. I hope they repent to God and to Sandra for their selfishness. I also hope they further her legacy by continuing her revelations and presenting them to the rest of the world. Her blood should not be shed in vain.

Dr. Sebi, a famed herbalist, went to jail for suggesting that he had the cure for AIDS. He was later released and then won his case based on facts. Using the medical records of his patients who had AIDS, he proved he could cure. And since native people are allowed to perform healing without interference from the government, he also proved that he had the right to practice traditional African healing.

Dr. Sebi is just one of many holistic herbalist doctors who have been persecuted through the courts for practicing healing. Others have been murdered for exposing the lies of the medical industry and revealing the true causes of cancer, AIDS, and other diseases.

Rapper and artist Tupac Shakur took a stand for black consciousness. He had a level of influence that would ignite others' awareness, from the hood to Hollywood. He advocated for racial harmony and tried to bring unity to troubled communities.

Almost every social interaction is floating on the surface of some wicked undercurrent that only the light of truth can expose. Avoid getting pulled down into the undercurrent. Instead, stay in the light.

Many people do not want to hear, know, or embrace the truth. Not only do they not want the truth, but they will seek to assassinate your character for giving it to them.

Although these kings and queen were despised and rejected of the truth they exposed and lived their fruit yet carries on.

Things Always Come Full Circle in the Light of the Truth
I went from being the beloved to being the betrayed. When I embraced the light of truth, it exposed what was in the hearts of people I was convinced had nothing less than love for me and had my best interest at heart.

Tonya M. Thomas

Once you've embraced truth, you must share it with others. But be sure you are a first-partaker. When you've known the pain of what truth can show you, you are then more compassionate toward others who have yet to experience it. You will be more careful, patient, and gracious while giving it to others. Please don't ever walk in pride and arrogance with your deliverance and don't ever forget that you too was "caught up". This is a journey not everything is an overnight miracle something's even you are coming out of darkness of, even myself I am constantly learning things that I had nothing less than total knowledge of and without hesitation speak on, the truth has shed light that I now have to reposition my stands on. In all we do we must have and show love even in our delivery of this powerful source of the "TRUTH"

Truth Even in Darkness
Sometimes strange but good things happen in the dark. I am often amazed by the revelation that can only be given in the darkest places. Just as a seed germinates in the ground in the dark, a child grows in the darkness of the womb. Don't be surprised if amazing revelation and truth about the core you, which are essential for you to embrace, come to you in the darkest places.

Almost every relationship requires compromise of some kind as the people involved grapple with the idea versus the facts of the relationship. In that struggle, we are sometimes confronted with the truth, but we may not want to accept it, so we press on,

Am I Your Enemy Because I Tell You The Truth?

pretending all is well and that we don't see the glaring facts that are alerting us to trouble.

Maya Angelou said it best: "When someone shows you who they are, believe them the first time." We often don't heed these words. We retreat into a cloud of denial, wearing blinders to the truth. But truth will always be your tour guide, if allowed, and can lead you away from toxic relationships and into ones that are fulfilling and effective.

Without truth, all relationships are nothing more than pretend. While those false relationships might lead to awards, money, and notoriety in Hollywood, in real life, they usually result in wasted time, frustration, sorrow, and pain.

It's perfectly normal to want to believe the best about others. We might even convince ourselves that we see great potential in them because it fits our ideal of who we think they are. But remember that potential and capability centers around an individual choice; and since God gave us free will, we are agents of choice.

So when people make choices we don't understand, we're often left disappointed because they didn't respond in "the perfect way," or the way in which we hoped they would respond. We are upset because our idea of perfection includes our own thoughts and plans about how others should act or the decisions they should make.

Once we've reconciled our ideas of perfection, though, we may have to admit that there's nothing left for us in the relationship. Sometimes the best and only thing to do is to walk away, be real to yourself, and admit that your staying in it a day, an hour, or a second longer is not going to change things for the best. Leaving becomes your therapy. Choose the lesser pain, and live. Be honest with yourself, and see if this person is worth any more of your expensive time.

Remember that you set the standard for how others treat you. You also control how others affect your life simply by guarding what you allow to come into your heart. The Scripture says, "Keep your heart with all diligence; for out of it are the issues of life" (Proverbs 4:23). So watch and pray. Stay vigilant at all times.

In my own life, I've been guilty of being a conqueror of the big things while being a slave to the small things. I have preached messages to great congregations, laid hands on the masses, prophesied, and seen signs and wonders, only to find myself the next day getting angry with a store clerk. I have said no to men I knew I wanted and felt would be great assets to me and to my son, but in the midst of transition found myself saying yes to fools for a space of time.

I have come to the conclusion that while I have been an overcomer in many areas of my life and won many great victories, there are still places where I haven't been as successful. Temptation is never separated from enticement and desire. The problem is not who wants me or how many want me. The problem lies in who and what I'm attracted to, because it's my weaknesses that the enemy will exploit to bring me down.

Am I Your Enemy Because I Tell You The Truth?

That's why I have to watch and pray. That's why I have to be extremely vigilant in all things. I don't want to give the enemy any leverage to use against me to stop my progress.

CHAPTER 3
Be Yourself Because Everyone Else Is Already Taken

The world is missing a harmony that would otherwise be a sweet melody for the lack of your authentic you. So be yourself so the world can complete its harmony.

People have always called me a risk-taker, but I've just thought of myself as living my life to the fullest. While to family and friends it seemed as if I was exposing myself to any peril or hazard without thought, I was simply pushing the boundaries because I'm never satisfied with the status quo.

With all the things I've had to go through, I refused to take the path of least resistance or the easy way out. Often, I chose the road less traveled, knowing that I would face uncertainties, but it was part of my strategy to live my life with no regrets.

As a child, I never liked bullies, my advocacy started very young. I not only fought for people and my own siblings, I would attempt to make permanent change to many of these isolated issues. I knew then that my life would never be humdrum and ordinary. But to me, it was never about how well I fought but, more importantly, what I was fighting for.

As a native of Detroit, I saw the enormous changes that my hometown underwent as the factories and other businesses closed

Tonya M. Thomas

and more and more people fled to the suburbs, the drugs that literally took our city to a downward spiral. You must understand that Detroiter's by nature are relentless we are built with an unspoken strength of tenaciousness, resilience, and fortitude that can't be reckoned with. There is pride that goes deep within the city despite of its challenges, because shift happens to us all and all cities.

Although I am familiar with the depravity that surroundings it, I also have had the privilege of proudly experiencing communities filled with all working class people who took pride in their homes and neighborhoods. I've witnessed and experienced more black owned businesses in my community as well as black leaders in our government in the City of Detroit that were both conscious and at one time had strong integrity and pride. There was a time when Detroit was the world "Oasis" it was so fertile with many opportunities, that it became the trendsetter for the world; with its car industries, fashion, music, and amazing culture. Many diverse people came from all over to take part and thrive off of its riches. These extraordinary people, left the mundane and decided that everybody "except me" is going after the joy of something better. And surely, for a space and time "Detroit" was that better. People became home and business owners, dreams were realized, chance & opportunity became whatever one can desire.

So yes, just as the bible will ask "can anything good thing come out of Nazareth"? Yes, plenty of good came out of Detroit. And yes, Martin Luther King jr. dream in many ways were realized. I grew up with and went to school with diverse group of children,

Am I Your Enemy Because I Tell You The Truth?

our teachers, police officers, and leaders were diverse and well received from everyone. The sense of peace, harmony, pride, and unity was felt and practiced in my era in Detroit.

Because of the shift, I felt a sense of urgency to serve as a solution and make things better in any way. I have always felt that it was a moral, cultural, and spiritual responsibility to respond with positive, effective, and righteous change in my space of life.

Sometimes in the darkness of pain, disappointment, and heartache, disillusionment sets in, and we accept the enemy's lie that this is it, this is the best it will ever be. But what power does he have to tell you that? Who wrote that script?

Each day, scripts are thrown at us daily, but you do not have to accept them. Distinguished actors reach the height of their craft because they learned the power of hewing their crafts and talent and to say no to some scripts, while saying yes to others. Their experience in the industry gives them the wisdom to know which scripts will probably be best for them to take, and they know that others will be failures.

Remember, like a seasoned actor reviewing scripts, you always have a choice. After expounding on all that the Lord had done for them, Moses spoke to the children of Israel and challenged them: "I have set before you life and death, blessing and cursing: therefore choose life, that both thou and thy seed may live: that thou mayest love the Lord they God, and that thou mayest obey his voice, and that thou mayest cleave unto him: for he is thy life, and the length of thy days" (Deuteronomy 29:19-20).

Tonya M. Thomas

To the next generation of Israelites, Joshua told them to choose between the one, true God and the idol gods of foreign nations: "Choose you this day whom ye will serve" (Joshua 24:15).

God created us as freewill agents, but we also have to accept that with free will and choice come consequences. Choose life, for that end is life and peace. Choose sin, and that end is shame and death. Although God always wants us to choose Him and choose life, ultimately, the power of choice lies within us.

Growing up, I was told that I would never have anything, never go any further than where I was, and that I didn't deserve better. But it was hard for me to receive that. I always colored outside the lines, so I didn't conform to the norm because I knew I was wired differently.

Although I was deprived of many things, I went on my way to expose myself to other things, beginning with books, I thank God every day for libraries. Books took me to places and allowed me to experience vicariously those things that were forbidden to me. More importantly, they allowed me to escape, if only temporarily, my dismal surroundings. They allowed me to see the possibilities life had to offer. Once the seed of hope was planted by what I read, I developed the optimism that someday I would escape poverty and dysfunction and be more than my circumstances.

I didn't have parents who encouraged me, guidance counselors that advised me, or life coaches that gave me pep talks. But God gave me a drive that could not be crushed by depravity, abuse, or negativity. I wanted greater, and God fed my faith to do it.

Am I Your Enemy Because I Tell You The Truth?

If you grew up with loving parents, thank God for them. I didn't have that. I merely survived my childhood. Instead of nurture and encouragement, my parents were dream-killers and spirit-crushers. If I had believed all the negative things they said about me, or their lack of motivation of good things, I would have faltered a long time ago and would have lived a life of regret.

I did however had an absolute wonderful grandfather, Clinton Hall Sr., who always told me I could fly. He picked cotton as a child and didn't realize his all of his own dreams. But he loved me and wanted me to go beyond what he understood. He supported every business I opened, every speaking engagement.

I had, and every award I received. He was right there, loving and supportive, his chest sticking out with pride for his granddaughter, Chicken, as he used to call me.

My other grandfather, Thomas McMichael, was also very supportive and a strong influence on me. He didn't waste time telling me what I couldn't or shouldn't do like my grandmothers did. He didn't talk negatively to me. Instead, he loved me unconditionally and stood up for me when I needed him to.

Even though the naysayers gave me all kinds of reasons why I couldn't do something and told me what I wasn't, I was fueled even more to accomplish my dreams. The more they talked, the more I wanted better for my life. With the grace of God, when I did reach my goals, I would go further beyond their expectations as well as my own.

Tonya M. Thomas

So without money, help, encouragement, or support from the naysayers, I've opened and operated my own business, held annual huge expos & seminars, created effective community initiatives & forums, bought houses and cars, ministered to the homeless and those in prison, rubbed shoulders with famous and influential people, became a sought-out speaker, obtained college degrees, gotten married, and so much more. And now I'm writing my first book, and I know God's not through with me yet

Who Told You That?
Who told you that you can't do better? Who told you that you're not smart enough, cute enough, tall enough, white enough, black enough, cool enough, or strong enough? Maybe someone told you that you will always be like this; that this is all there is; or that there's no life after prison, abortion, or divorce. Did they tell you that you'll never get married, no one will ever love you, no one even likes you, and that everybody hates you?

Who said that information from the media is always right, right is wrong, and everything your family said was wrong is right? Maybe they said more money, more happiness; or perhaps they said more money, more problems. Have you heard that all men are dogs, all women are hoes, all white people are racists, all black men are trifling and don't take care of their children, and all black women are angry? Only Europeans are business owners and not minorities, minorities only make good workers and not good leaders?

Am I Your Enemy Because I Tell You The Truth?

Maybe someone told you that all church people are kind and without fault, all policemen are brutal, all Latinos are maids and crop workers, all black people can dance, and that all white people can't dance. Who said that all young black men love rap and all young white men love Wall Street, all Lebanese are Muslim?

Who said keeping it real will not keep you broke and all Northern especially Detroiters are dealers and killers? Whoever said that all married people are happy and single people unhappy?

Who said that skinny people have more fun, blondes are sexier, and sleeping with many women solidifies your manhood? Calling a woman a "Bitch" should be acceptable along with using the word "Nigger" in any way is cool? , You are too old to go back to school?

Whoever told you that only women suffer from molestation and not men as well? Who convince you that if another man have sex with another man that whoever is on top is not considered gay?

You should compromise your freedom on behalf of someone else though you are innocence-"snitches get stitches" and you will be called a bitch, taking the blame and going to jail you will become somebody bitch? Asking for help makes you weak? Not initiating the gossip makes you not the gossiper, your silence in the lie keeps you from being a part of it? Not confronting is the way? Stealing is not a sin?

Who told you these lies? I have to stay I have nowhere else to go, besides he/she beating only means they love me? Seeing a psychiatrist makes you crazy?

Tonya M. Thomas

These lies, based on myths, stereotypes, and ignorance have shaped our society and caused us to be divided and not trust one another. You cannot define the valuable you by how people respond and think about you. They also stunt our growth and development in our relationships and interactions with others. We all must confront these vicious lies and call it all lies and in exchange speak the truth! There is power in your belief and your stand. We need God to heal us, and we need truth!

Coming Up Empty

After Jesus' resurrection, he made several appearances to his disciples. One such appearance occurred on the shore when the disciples were fishing. At first, they weren't even aware that it was Jesus. But after a night of not catching any fish, Jesus appeared and asked, "Children, have ye any meat?" Of course, they didn't, so He told them to "cast the net on the right side of the ship, and ye shall find" (John 21:1-6). They obeyed Him and caught so many fish that they couldn't bring them on board the boat.

Like many parents who have to give their children instructions and tough love, Jesus had to tell his disciples exactly what to do to catch the fish. Although Simon and his brother were professional fishermen, they still had wasted a whole night without catching even one fish. It wasn't until Jesus appeared and told them what to do that they were successful.

As parents, we may see our children stumbling trying to figure out a matter and not relying on what they've been taught in the love of truth. Often, these difficult times are normal opportunities that will further build and shape their character. But it's hard for parents to stand by and watch their children stumble in darkness while they learn the hard lessons of life. They've tried and tried but have come up empty.

But we are often guilty of doing the same thing, and our heavenly Father lovingly asks us, "So how's that working for you?" He watches as we run into the same brick walls over and over again. We make the same mistakes. We enter relationships with the same type of people, settle for the same poor career paths all while pursuing misguided fortune, go after goals ill-prepared, set out to be what others want us to be, try to please people who will never be satisfied; and then wonder why our nets are empty. Instead of relying on the wisdom of the Father, we rely on our own strength because of our education, know-how, talent, experiences, or connections. But then the Father tells us to cast our nets in a place we might have already tried or in a place we never thought to try, and before we know it, we are overwhelmed by blessings.

Why, God? Why Me?

When we've gone our own way long enough and God asks, "Have ye any meat?" we have to put our pride aside and answer truthfully: "No, I have no meat!" Just as with the disciples, some of whom were professional fishermen, you may have perfected your skills and have been thinking for yourself a long time. Perhaps you've mastered your techniques on handling your life, and you don't leave anything to chance. Over the years, you've acquired a measure of "meat": money, relationships, fame, affluence, or power.

But for all of the things you've acquired through your skills, talents, and abilities, you've also found that none of those things came without cost. And that cost can turn into a burden, which makes the joy of having them fleeting and not worth all the bother.

But when you give it to Jesus and hear and obey His commands, you'll see that the outcome is different. When the disciples were honest and admitted that despite their best efforts they had caught nothing, they humbled themselves and were then able to hear and obey Jesus' voice. They cast the net on the right side of the ship just as Jesus instructed. Their "then" became their "now," and they had an abundance and an overflow that they could not even contain.

When you have time, read the rest of the story of Jesus' appearance to the disciples (John 21:9-13). You'll find that not only did Jesus allow them to partake in His miracle, but He also prepared a fire and roasted bread and fish as they came to shore.

When you do things all your own way, you'll end up circling around and around, getting nowhere. You're like a plane waiting to crash. You're trying so hard to survive and work things out on your own, but you don't realize you're wasting your time.

Jesus will bless you, but he will also allow you to have a safe and smooth landing. In addition, He has prepared a place for His prepared people. His blessings are those that "maketh rich, and he addeth no sorrow with it" (Proverbs 10:22). He will bless you

Am I Your Enemy Because I Tell You The Truth?

with your needs and many of your desires, and He will go over and beyond your expectations.

Jesus is the original "Wower." If you ask for a job, He can make you the CEO of the company. If you ask for a three-bedroom house, He can give you a six-bedroom house. If you ask for a soulmate, He can give you the most attractive friend, prayer partner, and encourager you have ever laid eyes on. If you ask Him to improve your child's behavior in school, He can make your child the valedictorian.

If you pray for your mate to be saved, He can save him to the point where he beats you to church and studies the Bible more than you do. If you ask for a better bus route, He can bless you with a Bentley. You get the picture.

"According to your faith be it unto you" (Matthew 9:29). The question is, How much can you handle? Do you have great capacity? Some people have little capacity, while others like me have great capacity. The capacity of my faith doesn't make me superior, though.

I like to think of it this way. I have a gallon-sized life, while some people have pint-sized lives. So I can pour what I have onto you, but you would be overwhelmed because your capacity is much smaller, and you're unable to handle all that I am able to give. So when I share what I have, I can only give in the measure that you have capacity for. All gallon-sized people think alike, and pint-sized people think alike. Because I think big, I'm able to do big things. The same is true for people who think small.

But God has an unlimited supply of blessings for all of our different shapes and sizes of capacity, insuring that our blessings will be "exceeding abundantly above all that we ask or think" (Ephesians 3:20). We are joint heirs, equally given the inheritance. So obey the Lord, and put your net on the right side, Jesus' side, and let God wow you!

The most important and rewarding decision you can make is accepting the Lord Jesus Christ as your Savior. This relationship comes with the benefit of our Lord equipping you and giving you His Comforter, the Holy Spirit, which is also the Spirit of truth: "And I will pray the Father, and he shall give you another comforter, that he may abide with you forever; even the Spirit of truth; whom the world cannot receive, because it seeth him not, neither knoweth him; but ye know him; for he dwelleth with you, and shall be in you. I will not leave you comfortless: I will come to you" (John 14:16-18).

How many times have we needed the Spirit to work in our lives? Usually, we try to do it on our own first; but then when we run out of ideas to throw at our problems, it's then that we are willing to yield to the Spirit and let It work.

I admit I've waited until I've exhausted all my resources before I cried out to the Lord. It's not because I think I have all the answers, but I've had to be independent and not rely on anyone else––which wasn't by choice but by force. So it's a knee-jerk response for me to try to solve my problems and everyone else's.

Am I Your Enemy Because I Tell You The Truth?

But that's worked against me more than it's worked for me. I've been the "shero" so many times that other people think I don't need anything and have unlimited amounts of strength. They think I'm a superwoman, but I always remind them that even superheroes are susceptible to some form of kryptonite and can be weak and vulnerable.

Before I am a lawyer, teacher, single parent, pastor, leader, boss, daughter, evangelist, and prophet, I am a child of the King. Because that role has priority over any other, I now have the ability to become all of those other things and be the best I can be.

Life Without Me

In retrospect, I look at my life and marvel at what I've done, where I've been, and who I've become. As a multidimensional woman, fully convinced of accomplishing what appeared to be unobtainable goals, compassioned about the saving of the human race, truly believes in love without a limit.

I will fight with the quickness for the underdog. Sometimes I think I might just be the next Harriet Tubman, a phenomenal woman and leader. I don't mind following, but I refuse to follow the blind or any other nonsense. It's not hard to guess that I'm assertive, will get the job done, and will put a 100 percent into whatever I do. My anger that is employed by my compassion for fairness and justice for the human race can be explosive and costly.

I don't believe in impossibilities, and I certainly do not believe in the words *cannot* and *no* when it comes to positive goals. I'm fearless, and I know for a certainty that it is only the Lord Jesus Christ and His grace that have gotten me through thus far. I have my own swag. I'm a risk-taker, I'm goal-oriented, I'm independent, and I'm self-motivated. I love without limit and enjoy and embrace the kid in me. I'm a strong nurturer, I know no stranger, and I'm self-sacrificial to others while oftentime struggle to take care of myself.

But after summing up all I believe myself to be, I strive to live life without me. When I say life without me, I mean living without my ingenuity, intellect, and experiences and without my ways, my thoughts, my habits, and my calculated measures of handling things. Instead, I have been thrust into the center of God's will--His plan, His move, and His objectives.

The most difficult part of transitioning from my life with me to my life without me was my resistance to letting go of what used to be to accepting what was always meant to be. *Life* by definition is the condition that distinguishes animals and plants from inorganic matter, including the capacity for growth, reproduction, functional activity, and continual change preceding death.

When I came to the end of myself, I simply surrendered with the certainty that God would catch me. In addition, I accepted that the time and space I was leaving behind had rendered all it could, and it was now time to go forward into a new season.

The great thing about surrendering to God's plan is how free I feel. The burdens have been lifted. Now I can rest and relax and feel carefree! I don't have to worry about what's coming next. God

Am I Your Enemy Because I Tell You The Truth?

already knows that and has planned for it, so I don't have to. He's taken care of everything. I feel almost like a child again!

Talk to children who are well cared for, and you will find that they're not concerned about how the mortgage is going to be paid or where their next meal is coming from. They don't seem to have a care in the world because they trust their parents to take care of them.

If you grew up like I did, you may not be able to relate to living a carefree life as a child. Perhaps you did worry about being able to eat or where you would sleep. Maybe your parents failed you and didn't take care of you as they should have. But now you can know the Lord Jesus Christ as your Father, and He is the best Father in the world! The psalmist said, "When my father and my mother forsake me, then the Lord will take me up" (Psalm 27:10).

Now that I am in relationship with Jesus, I no longer have to concern myself with worries about my future, which gives me such peace and serenity. I'm so grateful for that. To be honest, even when I was worrying and getting stressed out, I was never smart enough or clever enough to figure it all out. Other times, I was thrust into the role of problem-solver by selfish and broken people who expected me to solve their problems as well as my own.

I am not bitter about my past. Instead, I've reached a place of healing because I have an understanding, loving, and caring Father who has helped me to forgive them and move on.

When I surrendered, the measure of release did not come without a cost. Total submission came when I put my pride aside and realized that I don't have this. But it also came with a sweet liberty. Our human will can often keep us from a life of bliss and abundance if we don't put it in check and, ultimately, kill it. Jesus said that He came so that we "might have life, and that [we] might have it more abundantly" (John 10:10), so it's the Father's good will and good pleasure that we have an abundant life, not a life filled with hardship and pain because we refuse to live our lives outside of Him.

Be Who God Created You to Be

"You like me, you really like me.." Sally Fields

Sally did not know many of us loved her long before she received the award. But society has a charge on us so strong that until we meet their expectations and acknowledge us we may buy into the lie that their approval solidifys who we are or should be.

We live in a society that throws a lot of images at us. We're bombarded with giant billboards, TV commercials, YouTube ads, movies, Instagram, Facebook, and a swirl of other places where we are told who to be, what to do, what to look like, what to eat, what to like, what to wear, and so on and so. If we're not careful, we can let the pressure get the best of us.

Even when we are around our family members and friends, we can often try to be like them instead of being who we should be. Association can bring assimilation, which means that if you hang with certain people, you will become like them. Think of it this

Am I Your Enemy Because I Tell You The Truth?

way: It's like getting in the hog pen to help the hog, but instead of helping the hog, you become like the hog.

Sometimes you just have to brave the critics and be your true self, the self that God created you to be. Don't be afraid to be criticized because your uniqueness is what is needed and will be where you will find your strength.

Appearances are fleeting and mean nothing in the long run. People get caught up in their careers and let them define who they are. They believe that the more money they make, the nicer their office is, or the more contacts they have on their phone make them more successful; and they will not rest until they have achieved all that and more.

I'm not discouraging success, but I'm encouraging you to discern the difference between what really matters and what doesn't. There are those who will lie, cheat, steal, and kill for what they think is success. But instead of fulfillment and satisfaction long-term, they come up empty, desperately trying to fill that emptiness with something––anything––so they can feel whole.

They believed the lie that all that glitters is gold. They fell for appearances and what looks to be successful. But all of that has failed them and left them with nothing. True success is you at your most authentic, highest, purest form able humbly to create inhibited with unchained liberty, It's the authentic you.

You might have heard the expression "Image is everything," and to many people, that is true based on their idea of truth. So they scratch and claw for the notoriety, cars, the houses, the vacations, the clothes, the shoes—whatever their definition of looking good and being successful might be.

If a paycheck and what it can buy, if climbing the ladder of success, or if making the list of all desired achievements are your only goals, then all you have had up to this point is a cheap existence. It's cheap because existing alone only addresses the air you are privileged to breath. But operating in anything less than what you were born to do and to be is selling yourself short and depriving the world of what you have to offer.

But you may say, "I have invested so much into this. I don't know anything else, and my lifestyle depends on me doing this." If that's the case, then you've taken the cheap route. In short, you have sold out and bargained down your value, expertise, intellect, skills, and talents. Even worse, you have wasted your most valuable commodity: time.

Never fear, though, because truth is here to save the day! You can still get back on course. It's simpler than you think. It's harder and more challenging being anything else than your authentic you, so returning to who you really are is easier for you in the long run.

When you give up the fight to be anything other than your authentic self, you give up all the behavior that goes along with that. Instead, you bear the beautiful fruits of the Spirit, which inevitably will reproduce of its own kind. You must choose the fruit you desire to bear, but keep in mind that your fruit shall remain, so why not choose the fruit that keeps on bearing even when you are gone? That's what my son Calvin did, and that's what other great

Am I Your Enemy Because I Tell You The Truth?

people did, such as my grandfather Clinton Hall I, Mother Teresa, Bishop Gilbert E. Patterson, Bishop David Ellis, Martin Luther King, Caesar Chavez, and Gandhi, just to name a few.

As a child, Shirley Temple was not blond, and she didn't seem to fit what Hollywood was looking for. But she stole America's heart because she was a gifted little girl with an infectious smile, and she left her mark on the film industry. In 1969, as an adult, Shirley Temple Black stepped outside of Hollywood and began her diplomatic career with an appointment to represent the United States at a session of the United Nations General Assembly.

My homeboy the Great Judge Greg Mathis, came from the tough area of the city of Detroit starting out as a fatherless kid from the projects to becoming a class act and one of the most popular and my absolute favorite judges this world has ever seen. What's most interesting is **he** is who **he** is.

Be brave, and be yourself. Be the self that God created you to be. You might as well because everyone else is taken!

CHAPTER 4
To Learn From the Past Is the Wisdom of the Future

History often repeats itself but with a different response for its time.

The Sins of the Father Are Visited on the Children

A healthy approach to the past is gleaning from it what you can to ensure a successful future but leaving it, as it should be, firmly in your rearview mirror. However, some people can't leave the past behind. Instead, they carry it, like a huge sack of dirty, rotten, dripping garbage, on their backs all the time.

Because of this foul garbage, they're unable to move forward, improve themselves, or have normal relationships. They harm themselves, their families, and everyone they come in contact with. It's especially true in families.

If you had a loving, caring, protective, and nurturing mother, you probably can't fathom what it's like to have a mother who was none of those things. As I share with you the things my mother did to me, you might have a hard time believing it—I know I do. As a mother myself, I would never have done to my son the things my mother did to me.

I suffered greatly at the hands of my mother. All of her rage and insecurities bled out into our relationship, which was dysfunctional from the start. Growing up, I didn't know what "normal" felt like, so instead of us playing our mother/daughter roles, everything was somehow switched around. I ended up being a "parentified daughter," which means I was the "mother," and she was the "daughter."

The road between a mother and her daughter is supposed to be, for the most part, a one-way street, with support flowing from the mother to the daughter. Little girls are totally dependent on their mothers for support, especially emotional support.

But sometimes that one-way street takes a detour and gets turned around. When that happens, instead of the mother supporting her daughter, the daughter ends up providing her mother with emotional support long before she's mature enough to handle it. This role reversal is incredibly damaging to the daughter and can have far-reaching, long-term effects on her self-esteem, confidence, and sense of self-worth.

In her book, *The Drama of the Gifted Child*, Alice Miller describes this dynamic. She writes that once a woman has a child, without knowing it, she might feel that she finally has someone to love her unconditionally. This is especially true if the mother has unresolved issues with her own mother.

The woman now feels that the child can fill the needs that were unmet in her own childhood. This puts the child in an impossible situation because she is now responsible for her mother's well-being and happiness.

With the weight of my mother's needs on my tiny shoulders, I then had to learn to repress my own developmental needs in order to accommodate her needs. She wasn't mature enough to provide

Am I Your Enemy Because I Tell You The Truth?

a secure emotional base for me, so I had to provide one for her. Faced with such a monumental task, I had a choice: Comply and fulfill her needs or rebel.

This abnormal role reversal is dysfunctional because it exploited me as my mother imposed on me adult roles I wasn't equipped to handle. I became a surrogate spouse, therapist, and best friend, and I was robbed of my childhood because I had to grow up too quickly in order to try to heal my mother's brokenness.

My mother thrust me into her role, and I had to cook, clean, do the grocery shopping, and care for my three siblings. I was more of a mother to them than she was. I resolved their problems, enrolled them in school, helped them with their homework, disciplined them, and took them to the doctor. At the same time, I was my mother's best friend and confidant. It was so evident that I was the mother of the house that my siblings called my mother by her first name.

Recently, I visited a childhood friend of mine. As we were reminiscing about old times, she recounted one of her memories of me as a child.

She had come over to my house so that we could visit another friend. But when she arrived, I was cooking dinner. I fed my siblings and took food to my mother, who was in the living room watching soap operas. My friend was amazed at how authoritative I was with siblings, all of them obediently sitting down to eat and then helping me to clean up the kitchen afterward.

Tonya M. Thomas

Then my father arrived, and I demanded to know where he had been and shared the lack of groceries in the house and didn't let up until he answered me. All the while my mother was glued to the television watching her soaps. Now my friend was worried. She had never heard a child talk that way to an adult and live! But in just those few moments, she realized just how much of the responsibility of that household rested on my shoulders. She also understood why I was more of a mother to my siblings than my mother ever was. What she saw that day amazed and puzzled her, but it was business as usual to me.

What she didn't know was that my parents thought I wanted to take their positions in the family. They hated that my siblings respected me more than they did our parents. While they shoved their adult responsibilities on me, and I had no choice but to step up, they still wanted us to see them as our parents and respect them accordingly. All of which shows just how immature and selfish my parents were.

It was not unusual for our utilities to be cut off because my parents didn't pay the bills consistently. It wasn't that my parents didn't have any money. My father worked for Chrysler, and my mother worked at General Motors, both being well paid. So where was the money? It was on their backs or it was in the driveway.

If you walked into my parents' closet, not only would you see it crammed full of clothes, but those clothes would be of the designer variety. My closet and that of my siblings was pretty bare in comparison. My father drove a Cadillac, and my mother drove a

Am I Your Enemy Because I Tell You The Truth?

nice car, too. So from outward appearances, you would think ours was a happy, healthy, well-adjusted home, but you would be wrong.

Occasionally, my mother would decide to cook my father a steak with all the trimmings. My siblings and I had to make do with TV dinners, pot pies, or hot dogs and beans. Every now and then I couldn't help myself, though. I would sneak into the kitchen, open the oven, and steal some of the food meant for my father.

But those were good times compared to what usually went on in our house. My mother suffered from depression, and that was reflected in how filthy our house was. Even though I was serving as mini-Mom, I would get exhausted with how bad things were and couldn't keep the house clean. At times, our house looked like a scene from the biblical story of plagues that God sent on Egypt so that Pharaoh would let the Israelites go. But instead of frogs, lice, and locusts, we had roaches, tics, and mice.

When the electricity was off in the winter, we had to use kerosene heaters. Uncle Michael, my father's brother, would occasionally bring us kerosene because my father was in and out, so we couldn't count on him to bring us fuel. With no electricity, our refrigerator was useless, so we had a cooler where we kept milk, bologna, cheese, and ice.

After making breakfast for my siblings, I finally got a chance to eat. I was eating my favorite cereal, Raisin Bran, but I wasn't really paying attention to what I was eating because I was reading the newspaper. Suddenly, though, I realized something was wrong. After taking a bite of cereal, I found that one of those "raisins" didn't taste right. After examining my bowl, I saw three roaches floating in the milk, blending right in with the real raisins.

My parents were so into image and how things looked that they never shared with anyone on the outside just what was going on behind that front door. I want to believe that if anyone had known just what was happening to us that they would have tried to save us. Years later, I found out that many of my family members were aware of what was going on.

Once, my maternal grandmother came over and cleaned our house for us and then took my mother to the grocery store. My paternal grandmother told me that she and my aunts bought us clothes, but when they came to the house to visit, they saw our clothes lying on the dirty floor. They also noticed how nasty the house was. They vowed that since my mother didn't take care of the clothes they had given us and didn't keep the house clean that they would never buy us anything else.

My siblings and I had to suffer because my mother didn't take care of things. It didn't help that that same grandmother would lavish clothes on my cousins, even though their mother didn't always "keep things up." That didn't seem fair. But then again, she probably assumed that we had two parents making good money, so surely we would be OK.

I used to believe that my mother was the victim in our whole dysfunctional saga. She would regale me with tales of my father's infidelities, including all the gory details. Then she would put me

Am I Your Enemy Because I Tell You The Truth?

on surveillance duty, the cheat police, spying on my father and his whereabouts.

My mother coached me so thoroughly on my cheating father that I can now smell a cheater from a long way off. Unfortunately, she was so busy teaching me about cheating men that she never taught me how to recognize and appreciate a loyal, faithful man.

My mother's paranoia was not completely unjustified. My father was often guilty of exactly what she accused him of. He was careless and narcissistic, so much so that he slept with my mother's cousins, friends, and neighbors. He even brought women home to share my mother's bed.

Of course, my father's escapades didn't come without a price. He fathered several children by these women. Some were kept; some were not.

Like my mother, my father couldn't resist confiding in me the explicit details of his exploits. He told me that my uncle's ex-wife, my mother's older brother allowed him to use her house for many of his illicit affairs. He also said that he was able to do this because my former aunt didn't like my mother. I don't know how true any of this was, but it made me wonder how any woman could do another woman that way. Whatever happened to sisterhood?

Many times, my parents' arguing played out like major battles. One night, while my mother was at work, my father brought a woman to our house and had slept with her in my mother's bed, escaping just before my mother got home. My cousin, who was there to babysit us, saw it all. When my mother got home, somehow she knew what had happened, but she forced my cousin to tell her everything.

Oh, such weeping and wailing and gnashing of teeth! You would have thought it was World War III in that house! I ran to my mother's bedroom to see what was going on. She was crying loud enough to wake up my siblings. I found her there crying and screaming while she cut up my father's clothes and destroyed his eight-track tapes. I held her while she wept profusely, and I knew I had to find out where my father was––or else! She finally fell asleep in my arms, and then I left her to take care of my siblings.

So, yes, my mother was a victim to a certain extent. My father was unfaithful, and he was a master of manipulation. He dragged my mother all over the place emotionally, mentally, and physically. But my mother was his equal in the game of manipulation.

All while my mother had me on surveillance, I was doing it to earn her love and approval. It wasn't enough that I was making good grades at school or was on the honor roll. She would usually blow off my accomplishments and treat them as nothing. I received many scholastic and athletic awards, but she didn't care. I even had the opportunity to be promoted to a higher grade level, but she wouldn't let me.

But if, like a good soldier, I reported back to her with all the details of my father's activities, then I would be awarded with a touch and maybe a smile, all the things that children want from their parents. Even then, though, God put people in my path who would show me love and inspire me to do better.

Am I Your Enemy Because I Tell You The Truth?

I was blessed to have great teachers. Two of those teachers forever impacted my life: Mr. Barach and Mrs. Greenwood, both of whom taught at Pitcher Elementary School. Mr. Barach a Eurpan Jew, would often slip into his teaching life-skill lessons and social challenges with solutions. I remembered one day during class, way off from the course he asked "what color an I?" , " we the class answered emphatically white!", he then took a sheet of paper and asked "what color is this paper ?" " We exclaimed white!" , he then asked "does he and the paper have the same color? He later expounded on the facts of our differences that they all are beautiful and we also have more in common than we don't.

Mr. Barach will often attend my assemblies and award ceremonies as well as other bright students. When my name was called at our school assemblies, he would have a beam in his eyes and would rise to his feet, giving me the loudest standing ovation. He was the father I always dreamed of having.

Not only was Mrs. Greenwood a great teacher, but she was a passionate educator. She treated her students as if they were her own children, and I felt as if she were my mother.

One night, I was awakened by my parents arguing. My father had come home drunk at 5:00 a.m. My mother took his cane away from him, beat him with it, and then returned to her bedroom, locking the door and falling asleep. When it was time for me to go to school, I had overslept because of the chaos that morning.

I set out to school anyway walking in the rain, alone.

Tonya M. Thomas

Not only did I arrive at school soaked, but it was picture day. Mrs. Greenwood dried me off and gave me some dry clothes to wear. Then she combed my hair so I would be ready to have my pictures taken. All the while, she told me how beautiful I was and how proud she was of my assignments. Later, she paid for my pictures.

What a God we serve! He had me all along. Even in the midst of drama and confusion, God was taking good care of me! Thank God for good teachers, the ones who go over and beyond what's asked of them. The ones who recognize when a child needs that extra special bit of loving care.

My father wasn't the only one being unfaithful. My mother had had several affairs, too, one of which was with a married man named Mr. Jack. Since his wife was cheating on him, my mother tried to convince me that it was OK for her to see him. Somehow, my mother had convinced herself that Mr. Jack's marital problems made him a victim and that she was justified in seeing him. She even claimed that because of him our bills were paid.

Mr. Jack won over my brothers by buying them video games and name-brand sneakers. I, on the other hand, wasn't impressed. Despite my father's actions, I was protective of him and saw Mr. Jack as an intruder. I was looking out for my siblings, too. I saw how this man was trying to get on their good side by buying them things. And, believe it or not, I was also trying to protect my mother. She was a shrewd woman, but she was still somewhat naïve.

Am I Your Enemy Because I Tell You The Truth?

Operating under a double standard, my father couldn't accept my mother's infidelities. How he handled the situation would scar my siblings and me for life.

One night, my mother was getting ready to go out. She had combed her hair and put on false eyelashes, all while talking on the phone. My father stormed into the house in a cloud of fury.

A guy that my mother would do part-time work for as a secretary for his auto repair shop had a cousin who worked with my father, and he took great pleasure in embarrassing him in front of all his co-workers by telling everyone about my mother and his cousin my mother's boss and her was having some kind of affair. My father, nicknamed Superfly, had a reputation around the plant of being cool, and he was extremely popular, so he didn't appreciate his co-worker cousin making him look bad.

When my father burst into my mother's bedroom, he dragged her off the bed, leaving the phone behind. Then he beat her, all the while yelling at her and yanking off her eyelashes. I wasn't going to let him hurt my mother, so I ran at him and tried to tackle him. My sister, following my lead, did the same. My brother Taurus froze, but his scream could have shattered glass. That day my siblings and I innocence died never to return. What's interesting though I would revisit that same scenario while trying to assist in a family squabble, this time with my uncle Roger my father's brother and wife Bernel only this time their son Emanuel took the place of Taurus my brother their screams and tears would forever leave an imprint in my mind but that day for those two-would be kings, a part of them died.

Though my siblings and I survived our family household the ill-effect will certainly affect us all differently for each one of us possessed certain strengths that the other did not. My brother Taurus has always been the one of reasoning and patience he possessed both a nurturing yet protective quality he was truly a quiet storm none the less.

His calm yet passive aggressiveness and unassuming patterns one can often misconstrued his bold qualities. Like me though if you harm who he loves you will see a complete other side. I recall when it was rumored that my x-husband had physically abused me, both my brothers then living in Nashville and I Detroit.

I wake up one morning and the two of them, my other brother Tony are at my front door. I had not called them I had not made any claims of any sort, but Taurus who never misses a day of work and does not jump and travel without plan "heard" that his big sister was in need and he showed up instantly.

I also recall my being in the hospital and like a nurturing loving parent my brother Taurus stayed the entire time and slept in the hospital room. Though he was younger I can honestly tell you there were times where his strength, wisdom, and love has carried me and my other siblings.

When you are not properly covered or nurtured it can and will show up in other parts of your life and relationships. My molestation experience made me overprotective of both my siblings

Am I Your Enemy Because I Tell You The Truth?

and my son. That experience would later show up in my personal relationships with men particularly I was ever careful of trusting men whole-heartedly.

This was just one of many incidents that shaped my childhood. But I don't share these experiences with you so you will feel sorry for me. Neither do I tell you my truth so you think that that's all there is to my life or to yours.

Instead, I share these things to show you where I came from and to let you know that through our heavenly Father, there is hope! There is help! There is love! My parents were broken people in need of healing and deliverance. They hurt each other and their children because they themselves had been hurt.

Maybe you felt that same kind of pain, and perhaps you've found yourself repeating that pain in your adult relationships. You don't have to. Let the pain, shame, guilt, and dysfunction end with you. You don't have to perpetuate it. With the help of the Lord, it can stop today!

Picking Up the Pieces

If we are to claim our power as women, we must be willing to see the ways in which our mothers were to blame for our pain as children. As adults, we need to see how we are fully responsible for healing those wounds ourselves.

One of the powers of adulthood is the ability to create harm whether intentionally or not. Many mothers are unaware of the harm they do or choose to remain in denial about it, but they are no less responsible. Daughters must own the legitimacy of their pain, or they will continue to sabotage themselves and limit their ability to thrive and flourish in the world.

With the many different dynamics in my family's home, one that was ever so clear was the difference between the four of us. My being the oldest, my sister Tina, my brother Taurs, and the baby Tony. We had all different unique personalities but there was always a difference from our parents toward my sister.

So much so that my brothers drew a conclusion that they felt she had something on them. Strange enough it was quite noticeable in fact often blatant, the many differences. Some examples included but not limited to monies, disciplinary, and certain showering of gifts even with poor behavior. This became an unspoken practice that I guess in hind sight I did not give it much attention because my expectation of them had died so many years prior and they always had a way to stay in compliance of not being supportive of me.

My father would often say "she has a lot of problems and is the weakest one so we have to give her special care". At this time my sister did have a lot of issues that my brothers and I did not have. With challenges like constant hair loss, she was practicing self-mutilation, she peed in the bed until she was twelve years old, and she often had skin problems particularly strong acne. Yet, the though giving her a Barbie dream house with all the fixings, while our lights were off and giving my brother a couple of $3 cars and me a pair of shoes was sufficient and balance with 4 children.

Am I Your Enemy Because I Tell You The Truth?

This practice will follow in our adult hood, so much so where I get a phone call from my brother Taurus who was extremely hurt that I couldn't make out what he was saying but it concluded with he requested to borrow my other brothers Tony car while he was away. Taurus already being very independent it took a lot for him to ask they told him no but the following week Tina and her husband had it and later caused the car some major problems. My mother actually gave Tina a great portion of an inheritance that she received from her mother's step-mother, both for her home and other things. What's even worse they make and show the differences even with the respected kids of each of us.

My thoughts however ,the statement that my brother had, what is does she have on them? The question was both reasonable but it came from a deep place. When you see people giving special attention to a child, especially undeserving, this not a result of a"good grade", "behavior," because even towards them there was oftentimes not blatant disrespect and the lack of following orders, yet when my brothers would attempt to do anything remotely close to the wrath of God came down upon them. But being a now victim of molestation, and now knowing that my mother would go to any extent of keeping my father as her man, that even if it meant that he molested my sister she and he will cover it and move on.

It took an incident during one Thanksgiving that my sister would out of an argument with someone in our household that she began to scream and cry and go on to say that my brothers and I never loved her and that we always wanted her dead!!.

Tonya M. Thomas

Now I have to tell you that concerned me, because I not only prided myself on my ability to protect and show them love. In fact often more on her, because growing up she didn't have many friends, when our door will knock from our childhood friends very seldom would it knock for her. I have always saw her as a pretty little girl and will pour a little extra on her when she found moments of challenges, from protecting, providing, and building her up. I had taken her and given her the best all her time that even her few good friends would express their desire of me being their big sister. But when a seed is planted both my devil and the manipulator/molester all good can be evil spoken of. One of the many masteries of a molester is first convince the victim that they cannot go to anyone else. In fact, their first order of business is to destroy any communication lines to the outside of the trap that they have build, get you isolated that only they can come in and out at their leisure, Convince you that those who love you don't and they do, occasionally will they provide for you because at the end of the day even a good pimp has to make you feel a certain special way all while he is building his fortress. This will later explain why my sisters strong jealousies towards me would show with such strong intensities whenever my father was around.

 I recall visiting them once, because I moved out early on and my father , sister , and I was sharing and when my sister showed a strong detest over my father admiring something I had done it was as intense of another woman watching her man admire another woman. When recognizing it I and my father asked her what was

Am I Your Enemy Because I Tell You The Truth?

her problem she even went to greater heights because he did not validate her position but rather mines, and why did he do that" she stormed out of the room like a sulking wife, being showed up by the "high school home coming queen".

While this major dysfunctions that first has its breeding grounds never began on those surface incidents but rather, they are the fruits of some strategic planted seed that has been watered through-time. The nurturing or the lack thereof my mother plays the strongest role because she like all mothers, control the gardens. My father could only plant seeds she has to allow it to take root and bear its fruits. If you are a mother and you allow your child to be molested in any form, rather its by their natural fathers, uncles, cousins or otherwise. Shame on you, your children should never be the burning sacrifice to keep your men. You are both selfish and very wicked to afford your children to fulfill your desire even at the cost of their innocence. Lives have now between my family and many others because of the weeds that my mother and others mothers failed to take out of the gardens.

But fathers have much to answer for, too. Many men have been so negligent in their roles as fathers, protectors, and providers that some women have tried to replace them by using their children as surrogates. Women are starving for validation, approval, and recognition, which is a hunger a daughter just can't satisfy. Yet generation after generation, children have been forced to offer.

If we are to claim back our power we must be willing to see the ways in which our parents were to blame for our pain as children.

As adults, we need to see how we are fully responsible for healing those wounds ourselves.

One of the powers of adulthood is the ability to create harm whether intentionally or not. Many parents are unaware of the harm they do or choose to remain in denial about it, but they are no less responsible. We must own the legitimacy of our pain, or they will continue to sabotage ourselves and limit our ability to thrive and flourish in the world.

Permanent Decisions on Temporary Circumstances

As I reflect on my life, I can see where I didn't always live with the future in mind. There were times when my life was in survival mode. When I was in survival I was more focused on what I needed at the moment instead of stopping to ponder how my actions would affect my destiny.

After being divorced for almost three years, I met and befriended Nnamdi. When we started dating, I thought I had found a friend, confidant, and partner all rolled up in one. But because of all the changes I had gone through during a rather tumultuous divorce, I couldn't seem to let my guard down. I would not allowed myself to sacrifice or chance my emotional and heart place at that time.

Long before I signed the papers, I had already begun to grieve the end of my marriage. During that grieving period, I didn't recognize myself. I gained so much weight, and I was emotionally and spiritually run down. But after the divorce, I began to work on myself. I renewed myself spiritually, lost weight, and worked

Am I Your Enemy Because I Tell You The Truth?

and build myself up financially. Blessings were raining down, and doors were opening for me. So when I met Nnamdi, I wasn't looking for him.

I was just rediscovering myself, so I wasn't in the market for a husband, let alone someone who was 13 my junior!

As our relationship developed, however, I became afraid. Sometimes you could have wanted something so much and for so long that when it comes, that you have given up on the thoughts of it. It's really true that hope deferred really does make the heart sick.

I just laid to rest any thought of being in a healthy relationship. I just did not have any room in me to entertain the thought, I also had found contentment in my singleness, and I was actually very satisfied in my now "wholeness".

Then with no notice love came, and cubit shot me with a double barrel, but even then I did not allow it to penetrate. I was afraid though my season to experience love had finally arrived, but I didn't feel prepared.

It seemed our relationship had a life of its own. Despite our common attraction, charm, and engaging conversation, we weren't the ones who brought us together; divinity chose us. This meant that Nnamdi couldn't just handle me any kind of way nor I him. Just like with truth, it's so pure that it demands the authentic you to come forth and stay present.

During the course of our relationship, I saw him as someone I could spend the rest of my life with, but I didn't realize how much baggage I was still carrying. I was oftentimes more reluctant and will pull back, even when it was so great. I was just ultimately scared of letting myself go.

Nnamdi and I shared many moments that I thought were intimate, but I wasn't sharing myself fully because I was afraid to let my guard down. As we began this journey I quickly came to the conclusion that my emotional scars, were very much present. I now understand that my inability of releasing the old was now sabotaging my new. The lie would had its free-course in my life through the entrance of the door of fear. I would tell myself that he wasn't sincere, and my old mindset would kick in, with all its baggage, and I would sabotage our relationship time and time again. Although the part of me in relationship to he and I was not handled I rested in the other sides of me (that I had greater control) was flourishing well.

As a new birth of me was developing and unfolding, I was feeling better of myself with weight loss, back in school, actually making time for me and learning myself again. I'm now fitting some old clothes, at least the few I didn't give away. And without plan or timing the inevitable had occurred, I learned that there was just not a rebirth of me but a birth of children in me, I learned that we were pregnant.

I had just came out of a miraculous surgery, for which in itself was a tale sign that God was for me the universe align itself for me and my season was here. By this time my son and I was hanging out and I was accused of being his girlfriend (smile) with his fine self I couldn't say who made who look better. You see there really are some perks of being African American (smile) we really do age gracefully and when you add being healthy inside and out, that will just take your stock up very high.

The miracle surgery was this, I had gotten back to a dress size of 10 due to hard work, and proper eating, but I through my father-side grandmother, I inherited these breast, that let's just say you will never have to ask me "you have milk"? Besides Dolly Parton and I could have gone to the same lingerie store for our bras. With all the exercise and weights lifting I couldn't do anything with them.

So I prayed and took faith with works to have a breast reduction, though my finance could not be foreseeable to pay for such an expense and I had no medical it was certainly going to take a miracle from my father God. After doing the work and fasting and praying the doors open. Let me just say it is so true that "the blessings of the Lord truly maketh rich, and add no sorrow" Proverb 10:22. I was able to have one of the top doctors of all time perform this great surgery.

The treatment I experienced, the place I was placed was so plush, that Queen Elizabeth would have gotten jealous. To add the cherry on top of one of many great miracles is that, my son was by my side and he was the last face I saw before anesthesia and the first face I saw when I had awaken from the surgery being completed.

By that evening my father and brother was there, and many of my good friends. Now because, this was so private for me they had no idea as to what I was actually there for, they though it was some form of bad cold that led to bronchitis. There lies the other miracle, all of my life I can sign my doctor prep paperwork and never have to check off on any elements of any sort medically speaking I was blessed to always have a good bill of health, Thank you Jesus.

The day of my coming home from the surgery my son and I are coming home, little did I know we were not alone? I began to feel sick, I just concluded that it was the medication or something, but he had to pull the car over and I began to vomit profusely, not thinking anything of it at that time.

My than friend would want for he and I to go to this next level that required a level of commitment from me, that's when the fear came in like a flood. I began to avoid him, and tried to lessen our visits (or control) you see I too began to feel and desire him as well, but I also went into safe mode- safety and very guarded, I would try to push him away, the more I began to feel so vulnerable. Thinking I was ill from surgery I had recently had, I began to feel sick all the time. Finally, I was rushed to the emergency room, and the doctor told me, a 40-year-old woman, that I was 8 weeks pregnant with twins. Those two little heartbeats would forever haunt me.

Panic and fear arrested my very soul when I leaned on my understanding and the ideas of others. Nnamdi would have wanted the babies but I let fear overwhelm me. So I started avoiding him and manipulating our relationship in order to control my new reality. I went into survival mode to keep myself safe from any hurt. The more vulnerable I felt, the more I would push him away. Our coming together was so surreal to me, it was one I never experienced all my life. It literally required nothing of me, in fact it was as natural as me breathing.

There was no labor, no pretend, no efforts of any sort. We literally just vibe so strong that we stood outside of time. I have never been here, "who is this, who are you, where on earth have you came from". Are you my test or are you my future? I have certainly had my share of dating but this was not in the handbook, I had no page of reference. One because I did not see him right away. I looked at him initially as a safe friend brother like, great for pastime. I would later understand that he was of my time and for my season.

I literally gave into the idea that this was just a good time for me. I also let my own goals and financial position deceive me into thinking that the timing just wasn't right. When I drowned out all of that noise, I had a sense of peace, comfort, and joy. So when I was in the Spirit, the answer was clear and peaceful, but when I was in the flesh, the fear was real and tormenting. How selfish and foolish for I to challenge the Sovereignty of God and prevent the lives of those precious little ones.

Looking back, I think Nnamdi knew about the babies before I did. This brings me to my only point of reference was when I carried my son. My son's father knew before I knew.

Yes ladies men go through things when pregnant as well, in fact Calvin's father did more of the vomiting and sleeping than I did, he also had more strange cravings than I did and gained weight. With Calvin's father however, there was this sense of control it was if he was trying to trap me. Yes men, there are some men that would actually try to purposely and intentionally try to pregnant a woman, especially the one he wants to be with.

Nnamdi would called constantly, confused about why I wouldn't see him. But I continued to avoid his calls. Finally, I answered the phone. I listened as he drilled me with questions. I relented and ask him to come to my house. When he arrived, it seemed as if the babies inside me danced for joy when they heard his voice.

I immediately put on my mask so I could brace myself for whatever Nnamdi would say. I had convinced myself that he wouldn't be supportive. But after telling him about the babies, how shocked I was when he said, "I'm here, and we are in this together." But I couldn't completely let my guard down. I had to further test his love. I gave him all kinds of excuses as to why I shouldn't have the babies, including my age and my recovery from my recent surgery. But Nnamdi simply looked at me and asked, "What do you want to do?"

That wasn't supposed to happen! Nnamdi wasn't following the script I had written for him in my mind. How could he be so loving and supportive? Still in a panic, I answered, "I want an abortion." He paused and reluctantly said, "It's your body, and I will support whatever you want."

The enemy is a master at playing mind tricks and manipulating us. Although my boyfriend was doing and saying all the right things, I had convinced myself of the lie society tells all women when it comes to abortion, that men really don't want the babies.

Am I Your Enemy Because I Tell You The Truth?

So since I said it first about the abortion I don't have to get the greater blow of pain of hearing him say it first.

I told myself that if I wanted to keep our relationship then I had to make this sacrifice, and he would be fine with my decision. The enemy's goal is to trap us with our decisions so that we forfeit God's plans for us, which will leave us fruitless and unproductive for our purpose and destiny.

When we arrived at the abortion clinic, there was a lone pro-life protester, a woman, standing outside. Before I even got out of the car, I began to feel as if I couldn't breathe. I thought I was having a panic attack. With the protester's soft voice ringing in my ear, I ran into the clinic and straight to the restroom to try to calm down and get myself together.

It was all coming back to me. This experience was like déjà vu, another time when I visited an abortion clinic, when I was pregnant with my son, Calvin. Although his father and my mother were adamant that I keep him, I wasn't so sure. I had plans. I wanted to be a lawyer, move to Atlanta, get married, and then have children. At 17, I was trying to come out of a controlled environment of poverty, high crime, and unhealthy exposures. Life had already through many curves at me that I did not believe there was a God and if there was He really didn't like me. After all look at my highly dysfunctional family I came from, my molestation experience, and to top it off the first time I share my body consensually, I GET PREGNANT !!!!!, wowwwwww.

Tonya M. Thomas

I did not want to bring a life anywhere near this type of environment, I thought an abortion would be the only solution.

After getting pregnant with Calvin, my father took me to a clinic. But instead of a single protester, there was a large crowd of protesters carrying signs depicting vivid images of aborted babies. I was so terrified that I ran away crying and begged my father to take me home. I was totally traumatized. Life as I knew it had changed forever.

Weeks would go by and still being very perplexed I rose up some nerve to go to my father and tell him to take me again. He trying to comfort me said Ok, this time we went, there were no picketers. I thought it was fate, only to get there after signing in and waiting for 45 minutes, though it felt like 45 days. I was finally called back and after a thorough examination I was advised, that I was too far long and that I could no longer get a "normal abortion" but I was now going to have to have a "saline abortion".

A saline abortion is performed by injecting the caustic saline solution into the amniotic fluid that surrounds an unborn baby in the second trimester. The baby breathes in the fluid, which burns their lungs and scorches their skin, causing them to die within hours. I would still go through labor except I would be delivering a dead baby.

Studies has shown that some babies have actually survived saline abortions only to be transferred to hospitals to later die. There was a nurse, from Jacksonville Fl., witnessed the death of one

Am I Your Enemy Because I Tell You The Truth?

baby who was born after a saline abortion and transferred to her hospital. She shared:

"I worked the 11 p.m. to 7 a.m. shift, and when we weren't busy, I'd go out to help with the newborns. One night I saw a bassinet outside the nursery. There was a baby in this bassinet – a crying, perfectly formed baby – but there was a difference in this child. She had been scalded. She was the child of a saline abortion.

This little girl looked as if she had been put in a pot of boiling water. No doctor, no nurse, no parent, to comfort this hurt, burned child. She was left alone to die in pain. They wouldn't let her in the nursery – they didn't even bother to cover her.

I was ashamed of my profession that night! It's hard to believe this can happen in our modern hospitals, but it does. It happens all the time. I thought a hospital was a place to heal the sick – not a place to kill.

I asked a nurse at another hospital what they do with their babies that are aborted by saline. Unlike my hospital, where the baby was left alone struggling for breath, their hospital puts the infant in a bucket and puts the lid on. Suffocation! Death by suffocation!

Before I can say anything my father said NO, and let's go. I was in total agreement and thank God. It's amazing how God in His infinite wisdom and love will be so bold enough to set something's up just to bless me.

Thank God for Jesus, because God know I truly needed and loved to have been so privileged to have my son. God truly knows what's best for us.

Tonya M. Thomas

One decision to share what I thought was love, to my boyfriend before him leaving for school, though we had been together for a long time, cost me, so I thought. I would learn later that, my son Calvin was and is the best gift I would have ever received in life.

So as I sat in the restroom of the clinic, trying to calm down and thinking of the twins growing inside me, I was once again terrified. But I numbed my emotions so I could do what I thought I needed to do. I allowed myself to become an empty shell so I wouldn't feel anything. It's the same thing I used to do when I was a child and was being molested.

As I lay on the table, waiting for the procedure to begin, I felt as if my spirit had left my body. *This is it*, I thought. But the doctor stopped examining me and instead gave me shocking news. He told me he could not perform the abortion because of fibroid tumors. I had had fibroid tumors for a decade but never thought it would keep me from having an abortion. But the doctor informed me that the fibroids were placed so close to the fetus that he could not perform the procedure without injuring me. So the clinic refunded my money, and Nnamdi and I left.

Next, I visited my OB/GYN and told him I wanted an abortion. Being from Ghana, where all children are considered a blessing from God, he couldn't understand why I would want to get rid of my children. I gave the excuse that my age and the fibroid tumors were a problem, but he told me neither was a problem and that at my age it was even more of a blessing to have children. As for the fibroid tumors, they would make it impossible for me to have the

Am I Your Enemy Because I Tell You The Truth?

abortion. By this time Nnamdi came into the room he and doctor concluded that I cannot and should not have it. I assured them that I would not, only all along I was planning my next escape.

Not ready to give up just yet, I visited a third clinic. My best friend/my sister, Neolitha Byrd-Johnson, affectionately called Byrd, I shared with her what I was going through and needed her support, she agreed to support me. I knew of a place back home in Detroit, it was also Thanksgiving and I can have an alibi as to my going home (the devil will always give you a strategy/plan to destroy yourself). We arrived at the abortion clinic very early to avoid the picketers and soon as we got in the doors closed within 3 minutes there were picketers everywhere.

Once on the operating table, again, I made myself numb. As I tried to empty myself of all emotions, I lied to myself about how the timing just wasn't right for these children to come. I told myself that if I just had a little more time for myself, then Nnamdi and I could get ourselves together and *then* we would be ready, how selfish of me.

But before my plan could come to fruition, the nurse was helping me up off the table. With no compassion and ready to move on to the next patient, the doctor informed me that he would not do the abortion. Three strikes, I'm out!

Desperate times call for desperate measures and desperate people really do desperate things, and I was truly desperate. I asked anyone who would listen what I should do. After three attempts, I was out of options, and I was willing to do anything at that point. But with my "baby bump" showing, several people just bluntly told me, "Tonya, maybe it's not meant to be. Maybe you're not supposed to do this." Even the receptionist at the clinic said that in all her years working there, she had never seen a case like mine. She was also convinced that it was meant for me to keep the children.

But I wasn't thinking of my destiny and God's purpose for my life and the life of my twins. I let fear and desperation overwhelm me and saturate my very soul. I ignored all the advice I had heard and went back into the operating room and begged the doctor to perform the abortion. He cursed me out and told me that even if he wanted to, he couldn't reach the fetus because the fibroid tumors were surrounding them like a fence and that he, too, had never seen anything like that before.

I left the operating room dejected. The receptionist told me that there was one other option. I could take a couple of pills. *Finally!*

I thought. *Here was my answer.* I readily agreed and took one of the pills before I left the clinic. But before I could get home, Byrd had to stop the car because I was violently sick. The pill came back up whole and undigested. I thought my last hope was gone and lying on the side of the road in a pool of vomit.

Now broke, hurt, and confused, I forged ahead in desperation. I took the second pill, thinking that maybe, just maybe, something would happen. It did. I ended up in an ambulance on my way to the emergency room. The EMT, with tears in his eyes, held my hand. He told me that his wife had miscarried several years before.

Am I Your Enemy Because I Tell You The Truth?

Little did he know that I wasn't miscarrying, but I was deliberately trying to get rid of my babies.

When I finally got to the hospital and was stabilized, I told myself that if that final pill didn't work, I would keep the babies. Besides, they seemed to have my tenacity and perseverance and weren't going to go away quietly by my futile efforts.

The whole time I was in the hospital and received visitors and friends, I never told anyone what I had done. I didn't even tell Nnamdi at first. It wasn't until I got home that I finally broke down and told him. Needless to say, he was devastated. With my pregnancy now terminated, it felt as if part of us had died. That's when I entered a place of condemnation.

In this place, no one could save me. Calvin had always been my medicine. He could make me feel better even on my worst days, but not this time. Once I told my son, I asked that he and Nnamdi forgive me, and they did; but it was much harder to forgive myself.

My life has always been in this race, let me explain the best as I can. Since a child it seemed as if I did everything fast, without trying to compete with anyone it was as if I was built and wired to just be about forward moving.

I have always been and am very agile and getting things done. I already had walked by a different drum beat never initially was just built like that. I have been a workaholic grind was always in my DNA. The need to always keep it moving forward moving, grow & go, even at the expense of my own health, I never knew how to just be still……

Tonya M. Thomas

This perpetual cycle of never being able to truly count on anyone being groomed from childhood, I always had to get it done, by any means myself. Even when I would have major setbacks I would hardly have anyone telling me "you can make it" or get back up, try again, though I was telling everyone they could.

I have understand that in many instances because I was always the encourager people did not believe I needed to be encouraged. I was always called "she so strong, she is tough, she always has it together, that they felt I didn't need it. You can really with all your masks persuade genuine people who would really sincerely help you that you don't need their help.

That does not excuse the takers and thieves who will never show no level of reciprocity anyway because they are selfish to begin with, In fact, when they say how are you doing it's just a greeting, and the only time they will bless you is when you sneeze and even then they saying "God Bless you", because they will not nor plan on ever blessing you.

The fibroids by this time were still growing leaving me with an appearance as if I was still pregnant. I searched and found this doctor like I was searching for a place to buy lunch or something, simply ridiculous on my part, desperation would do this. I had asked a couple of nurses at a nearby hospital in my community the three people I had asked 2 were nurses at the hospital and 1 was a receptionist, they were all white not that, that would have matter for any other reason. But the truth of the matter Fibroids are largely known in the African American women culture. Each

Am I Your Enemy Because I Tell You The Truth?

one of them had different types of medical attention from him, but what they all concluded was that he was nice.

I allowed nice to serve as my helm of decision because that was my strongest need at that moment. I not only was in a hurry to have some resolve, and not be daily reminded of what I had done, but I was also in desperate need of compassion, because I was truly beating myself up, condemnation had taken a very strong hold of me, my got-up and go had got-up and went and couldn't be found, I had taken melancholy to a whole new levels, It was literally killing me.

I would later set up the appointment with "the nice doctor" to have the fibroids to be schedule to be removed. The doctor and I had a very extensive consultation both on procedure and practice and more importantly my health.

The doctor was amazed of my age and thought I was in very good shape he did surprisingly asked me if I had ever considered a hysterectomy-and even began to share with what he thought were "the perks of having one".

The doctor would carry on like an insurance man, or car sales man, or a drug man trying to push his product onto me, just with a different style and method but with all the intent of and end result of making some more money. You see later on I would learn that not only would my doctor have made money from my surgery as he should of course, but there's a lot more money to be made with OBGYN's to perform that procedure, and inevitably prevent me from producing.

Tonya M. Thomas

This brings me back to a memory I remember once my mother and two of her friends having this very sensitive conversation of having some female medical conditions in the early 80"S, to conclude all three different women, having different bodies and challenges, having different all European doctors, yet all given the same diagnosis, with the only cure being a hysterectomy, which to me is another form of genocide.

They all under the "persuasion of their good doctors" accepted their prognosis and had it done. I only wondered if further investigation or another expert opinion might have been made, or and African Urbalist from an African descent would have done.

Yes, the truth is we are in such a Capitalist society that money rules and integrity doesn't, even at the expense of young women's health and their human and natural God given right to produce, money yet trumps.

Meanwhile the doctor's idea of perks were the following: "the perks of no longer having menstrual, the control of not having children, it will also flatten my stomach. I explained I was not interested I never had bad menstrual, in fact even at the age I was my menstrual were no more than 4 days with absolutely no cramps, my first two days were the heaviest and after which I had no issues of any sort. So we concluded with my having the procedure of the **fibroid removal only.**

But the drama wasn't over. I woke up from surgery only to find that I was having major complications. I knew something was wrong when I saw Nnamdi's face. He wouldn't tell me right away

Am I Your Enemy Because I Tell You The Truth?

what was wrong. The doctor had told him that what had happened was completely normal and necessary, but I learned later that that was a lie.

I was not recovering properly, and I tried to talk to the doctor on several occasions, but I was barred from his office. What was happening to me?

I learned that the doctor had used an old technique to remove my fibroids, and he left a large, ugly scar on my abdomen. It looked as if I had had a C-section. I was devastated.

The thief got in-with major Catastrophe

The unforbidden occurred with no consent, and raped and robbed me sparing no vengeance. As Whoodin would say "it was done so smooth it had to be a friend. " My good doctor-who coached me as a friend, performed the most incurable, regrettable, violent act towards human-kind h**e took of me.** When I learned of this major catastrophic event. I was 3 days of being home, it turned out Nnamdi had gotten the news the day of the surgery.

You see besides the great nurses that I was blessed to have he was by my side the whole journey. It got to the point that when they would ask for any of my medical questions or concerns he could answer, my parents nor anyone else knew more about my health than he did. Because of already having this most sinful act of committing to the abortion I never wanted anyone to know anything else relating to it, always with a lie there is this shame and need to cover something.

Nnamdi wouldn't share with me the news right away, which would later explained his depressed look partially including the loss of the children. This doctor explained to him that it was necessary, he gave me a hysterectomy, (this viscous act and that's what it was cut/remove a part of me, that only through a miracle act of God can replace),

Which I learned later was a complete **LIE**. Only after undergoing some major complications and this same doctor avoiding me, even went to the degree of having me barred from his office when I discovered what he had done. Dr. Louis Riley from Summit hospital in Smyrna, TN, not only performed this catastrophe to top it off he used old procedures that have not been used since the late 70's.

The only major surgery I've had was the birth of my son, and I had him natural. When Dr. Riley performed this surgery he cut my stomach, I look as if I had a C-section and the cut looked like it was done from someone who had palsy, certainly no one with a straight hand, what have made such crooked cut,This was only as prolific of who he was "a crooked doctor".

When there are many modern practices in place, now is simply performing a laser cut under the bikini line. After later going to Vanderbilt I met my (Angel) Dr. Norman, after seeing 3 different doctors who all came up with different prognosis, Dr. Norman came with the proper prognosis and solution. Dr. Norman had only been back in the states for 9 months with the intention of

Am I Your Enemy Because I Tell You The Truth?

only going back to Africa where he and his wife had decided for him to conclude his career/purpose there.

It turned out Dr. Norman had a prestigious record here in the Sates of being a top OBGYN, this European man had the soul of my grandfather, if I closed my eyes I swear he was my grandfather. He would later with his church go over for a short-time for ministry to Africa where he was successful for performing many successful surgeries for women, but was best known for removing fibroids there was a write-up where he removed a woman in Africa fibroid that was an estimate 9 pounds, people really believe she was pregnant.

He specialize in this area and when he came into my room for the first time I not only felt peace he gave me release, and immediately found what my previous doctor had done. It turned Dr. Riley did not even complete the surgery which explained the pain and the constant bleeding, he less than 5 minutes performed a practice that cured the problem.

I call him my Angel not only because of his ability to heal my body but to also heal my emotions. You see what proceeded me meeting Dr. Norman and the continual catastrophic pain was my going down on my knees and repenting to God of all I done, from the abortion, fornication, not trusting Him, flirting with fear, and not forgiving myself.

The visit with Dr. Norman (Angel) would forever change my life because he was not only an answered prayer but a expression of God's Grace.

I continue with Dr. Norman as my OBGYN doctor but as time would have it 7 months later he gives me the sad news. He had always shared his passion for purpose and the work he was doing in Africa, that he broke the news of he and his wife going back to continue their work there, he also explained how the traditions of the institution in the states was not working for him. Dr. Norman would also advised me to be careful when I do choose my doctor moving forward, just because someone is nice and smiling (this was the story of Dr.Riley) to you does not mean that they are the doctor you should have, he advised me to always pray and be still especially for making important decisions, yes my friend that truth came from my (Angel) Dr. Norman.

Stop Putting on Bandages on Where You Need Surgery
While I was so busy trying to manipulate and control my life, I didn't realize God's plans for me. In fact, the timing of my pregnancy and illness couldn't have been more perfect and divine. I was at a place of recovery and restoration, and more importantly, I was learning God as Jehovah, or God as my Father. I was discovering just how alive He is in my life.

More and more, God was showing me the Jehovah side of Himself. I had survived divorce, betrayal, and loss, but God Jehovah had protected me. Even when I was homeless, abandoned, neglected, and humiliated, He never left my son or me alone.

God had even provided me with Nnamdi, whose name means "my father is alive." God allowed him to become whatever I

Am I Your Enemy Because I Tell You The Truth?

needed: father, friend, confidant, provider, supporter, lover, counselor, corrector, and comforter. So why was I so afraid, and why was I tormenting myself? It was the pain of my unhealed past and all the lies that came with it. I had been plastering my hurt with bandages when I really needed the surgery of truth.

> *I'm learning to "master self" while rising*
> *from the ashes of madness.*
> *--Stanley "Tookie" Williams*

If you think about it, some of the bandages we use to cover our gaping wounds are drugs, sex, food, multiple relationships, work, shopping, and school—just to name a few. But no matter what we use to cover our past, we don't find true and lasting solace. We even use church to find that spiritual high, only to come crashing back down to earth, back down to our problems, with no true transformation looking and behaving like a walking contradiction.

Nothing we have will be a permanent solution. They're all just momentary escapes, so stop putting bandages where you need surgery! Slapping bandages on top of gunshot wounds doesn't heal them.

Confronting with truth and sheer transparency coupled with your placing your hurt to the only True Doctor, Dr. Jesus. He can really heal, transform, restore, and make you totally whole. With no signs of any ailment, in fact it would be like as nothing ever occur in your life.

Tonya M. Thomas

You also can't buy into the lie that it's too late, that you've gone too far, or that you've made too many mistakes for God to forgive. Know with confidence that God loves you. His grace and mercy are new every morning, and great is His faithfulness.

CHAPTER 5
Truth Should Be Understood and Lived to Bear Fruit

How can anything have meaning, substance, and consistency if truth is not its foundation?

That Prepared Me for This
Loyalty is one of my greatest strengths but also one of my biggest weaknesses. Perhaps my problem is not so much that I'm loyal, but it's what I'm loyal to that is the problem. If you have me for a friend, I am extremely loyal, regardless of your behavior. Even if you acted like a snake in the grass, I would still give you the benefit of the doubt, optimistically believing that you're really just a kitten longing to be healed and loved.

My loyalty has made it hard to choose the right man, the right friends, the right associates, the right business partners, the right employees, and the right staff. Again, I agree with Maya Angelou when she said, "When a person shows you who they are, believe them the first time."

God gives us common sense, but He also allows us to gain wisdom and discernment as we grow and mature in our relationship with Him. But, often, we ignore what God has given us and let our feelings, fantasies, and hopes of the ideal scenario cloud our minds and ignore the reality right in front of us.

Tonya M. Thomas

No one starts a friendship, a business, or a relationship with failure in mind. Usually, we all start out with a vision of what we would like to happen, hoping that reality will catch up with our hopes and dreams. So we wear our rose-colored glasses and fool ourselves into believing that all is well, when many times it isn't. So, we miss the red flags that we should be seeing. We don't see that the people with whom we've entered into relationships don't have our best interest at heart, and they certainly aren't loyal to us.

We then find ourselves partnered with people who would rather see us harmed than healed, who don't care if we live or die, as long as they get what they want from us. After that, we're disposable to them.

I am not telling you to cut off everyone around you out of fear that they are not loyal. God places people in our lives all the time who are there for a reason or for a particular season. Even the more difficult people in our lives can help us grow and learn tough lessons.

What I am saying, though, is that whenever you build anything, you should count up the cost. Jesus taught, "For which of you, intending to build a tower, sitteth not down first, and counteth the cost, whether he have sufficient to finish it?" (Luke 14:28). This means that every endeavor has a cost, so it is wise to think it through first so you won't run into problems later.

When I was a business owner, I had to comply with state laws and requirements for permits. I was required to demonstrate that I was able to handle anything that could possibly occur, including

Am I Your Enemy Because I Tell You The Truth?

hazardous and unforeseen challenges, and have the capacity to overcome them all.

When we build any relationships in our lives, we also have to make sure that we have contingency plans in place. If we thought through our decisions and prayerfully considered what we were doing before problems arose, how many frustrations and heartaches could we avoid?

Even if you have been hurt in your relationships, God will take care of you. It doesn't matter if others have intentionally set you up, hurt you, or been disloyal, God is there in every situation. It's comforting to know He will see you through any hurt or disappointment, but before we embark on future relationships, we can do as the writer of Proverbs suggests: "Trust in the Lord with all your heart and lean not on your own understanding; in all your ways submit to him, and he will make your paths straight" (Proverbs 3:5-6, NIV).

Being an African American woman has given me much credence on this form of life. First, I am African, which means my culture and origin play a role in my making from jewels of a rich heritage. Second, I'm American, so I am part of a powerful country that was bold enough and courageous enough to gain its independence from England and forge its own way in the world. Third, I'm a woman, so I'm privileged to have a womb that has given life. With my womb, I gave birth to a great man named Calvin.

Spiritually, I have given birth to ministries that have in turn birthed souls and brought them from lies to the undeniable truth.

Tonya M. Thomas

I have birthed men and women into their destinies through fasting and prayer. I've seen generational curses be overturned and turn into generational blessings. Through the grace of God, I have labored in prayer and birthed the deliverance of my natural father being delivered from drugs.

There are some disadvantages in coming from African American lineage, particularly what slavery did and has yet done to us. There are those who say that slavery was a long time ago. President Abraham Lincoln signed the Emancipation Proclamation in 1863, and President Lyndon Johnson signed the Civil Rights Act about 100 years later in 1964. But the effects of racism are still with us to this day.

This just goes to show the truth of how lies can have a ripple effect of brokenness and dysfunction long after the original misdeed. Lies can be perpetuated for generations upon generations with no end, if no one challenges the status quo.

Not everyone's story is the same, but pain is an equal-opportunity enemy. Slavery has done a number on African Americans, and healing is yet needed. More times than not, many people don't recognize the lies when they are indoctrinated into our psyche.

For example, there is a lot of negative imagery and myths about African American men. Think about healthy, strong black men who were enslaved to their masters. They were essentially stripped of their manhood and emasculated in front of their women and children. They had no choice as to where they would live or work.

Am I Your Enemy Because I Tell You The Truth?

Instead, they were snatched away from their families and taken somewhere else to serve at a new master's pleasure.

Once in a new place, they were forced to breed like animals so that the enslaved children would provide future labor for the master. No one cared about these enslaved men or how they felt. No one asked them what they wanted to do or if they wanted to stay with their families. They were shifted around with no more compassion than a load of unwanted clothes. They weren't allowed to become rooted or have a sense of belonging and foundation. They just had to make the best of a hellish situation and get on with life.

At least a rapist usually hides his face, but the slaves' attackers were out in the open. They also brought their friends as they took turns with enslaved women. The enslaved men had to emotionally detach to keep from caring or responding.

As the women screamed, they, as well as the children, looked to the men to do what should have come naturally––to protect. But though they may have longed to protect, they couldn't because they had been ambushed by the lie that they weren't real men and that they didn't have a voice. They were afraid of the whips and the lynch mobs. So the enslaved men became exactly what the masters wanted them to be: docile and nonthreatening. Their energy expended in jumping from one woman to the next and you don't think that that these practices are not relevant today. Not every proclivity from an individual comes from their immediate family, but generationally.

Tonya M. Thomas

Today, instead of the cotton field, it's the football field, the basketball court, or the golf green. Instead of palaces, they're in the penitentiary or in prison. Instead of the heat coming from sweating in the heat of the day in the fields, today the heat is coming from the systematic charges that are in place to keep these would-be kings in these places instead of the palaces they were intended to have and possess. I think of it this way: S.W.E.A.T is an acronym for **S**ystematically, **W**hite man, **E**radicated by design, **A**ssign for a bigger plan, **T**hreat.

Systematically. The agents/enemies are not limited to natural entities but are first spiritual, and they are not limited to race alone. Most times, the Judases are always close; slaves were initially sold by their own brethren. In fact, they are within kissing distance. The strategy was thoroughly and meticulously designed with certain people's demise in mind. This global design of having a certain sect or group in inferior positions has always been and will always be the goal.

This comprehensive design is a filter with reinforcements of bad imagery by the media, lifeless, and truth less people who are in the barbershops and at the BBQ joint. They're the men holding up signs for food on the streets, the drunkards on the corners, and the aimless pastors preaching in some kind of "ghost" every week. They're the comprising business owner selling anything for a profit to keep his master's company in business. They're the leaders refusing to take a stand publicly because they refuse to stand privately, humbly before the true lord of Lords, Jesus Christ.

Am I Your Enemy Because I Tell You The Truth?

Weakness. Just as the gym (location), the weights (substances), and the dumbbells (the work-out) are in place to exercise your body, some of these places you call home, neighborhoods (location), abuse of drugs (substances) are made in another country. They seem to make their way past secured borders and make it here though most of the distributors, who don't have a valid driver's license or ID, let alone a passport. Women, girlfriends, wives, other relations, friends, business partners, laymen, fan clubs, colleagues, children, countrymen, bosses, students, club members, baby mamas (the serious work-out).

Ambushment. It's always the unseen that you were not prepared for, the battle that confronts you with no sign, like those false accusers who were always lurking around the whole time (within kissing distance). Just ask Malcom X, Bill Cosby, and Tiger Woods. Did they see it coming?

Plenty of things are meant to ambush: predatory home loans, contracts with a lot of fine print, allegiance to the deferment of the entire family, casinos that make gamblers take that last hit, check-cashing places only in certain communities, liquor stores, and rent-to-own stores. Then there's that engaging beauty who captivates with her eyes, though it isn't her beauty that takes men out. That would be too easy, and most men are smarter than that. Instead, like Samson, men make the mistake of resting their heads in her laps. In other words, they drop their guard––represented by their intellect, instinct, and experiences––and then the enemy swoops in and handles them by pimping them out and making them his slave/bitch/dog. It's all part of the great lie.

Terror. Sketchy laws are enforced for some groups (slaves) while allowing other groups (slave masters) to their positions of power. The biggest terror is the lie, that this is the way it is and will forever be, the lie that "the Muslim race" was the terror of 911.

Falling on the support/need from a terrorist (slave master) indoctrinate you day and night that there is no hope and that you have no other choice but to submit. You may have hope as you look up to the stars and the sun, hoping for to disconnect from your present state to become what you are hoping for. But just when you think you can somehow make your desires and dreams come true and you're so close you can almost taste it, his whips comes down and pull at your flesh. The heat of the sun scorches the open wounds.

But the most serious wounds are inside and are coming from a place that neither you nor can anyone can see or touch in fact you're bleeding in more places that can't be seen. Your manhood is bleeding—those things that make you who you are and solidify your gender besides your penis and muscles, that thing that is your innate nature and longing to possess, that thing you are programed to become long before you say your first word, the thing your soul thirsts for. It is often mistaken for pride, mistaken for selfishness, mistaken for lust, mistaken for fear, but it is nothing less than your nature of being a dominant conquering creator of a **man.** And that is the need to plant your sperm/seed and reproduce your own kind.

Am I Your Enemy Because I Tell You The Truth?

It's not the lesser you, who they want you to become, but it's who you were created to be. Slavery stripped these great men and took more from them than 40 acres and a mule could ever replace. When a man is out of place and not in any place, a whole nation is lost for he is the leader. But even a leader has to have a Leader.

These slaves were led like cattle (handled like purchased goods with no soul) to function only according to the needs of their cowardly masters, who used the manhood of the slaves to conquer and dominate. This led to the slaves having a form of manhood but never the true power of a man. Real men would never subject any other man to do what only he should do for himself. A real man tills his own ground, sleeps with his own wife, creates and supports his own children. He never takes another man's wife or takes the fruit of another man's labor. A real man will create and cultivate his own destiny without stealing and taking on another man's journey so that he may make his own history for the world to embrace. Why not let the towel of TRUTH wipe your S.W.E.A.T away.

How Many Frogs Must You Kiss Before Getting Your Prince?

When I was younger, entering the dating world was a delightful experience. There were times in my early years I thought of dating like collecting data to gather this information that I needed to choose my propective. Like all information , good or bad, it was all very interesting. There were many times that my parents did not know who I was going to bring home for dinner because I did not discriminate. I have dated men who are Lebanese, Caucasian, Latino, Indian, and African. Their professions ranged from doctors, lawyers, business owners, students, and street pharmacist. I had the pleasure of sitting down to dinner with their families, I was most fascinated with their different lifestyles and how they communed with one another. It was then that I learned of so many expressions of the languages of love.

I vacationed with some of the men I dated. I took trips abroad, I went on ski trips, and I went boating and hiking. But my favorite excursion was horseback riding.

For me, dating involved welcoming another world of wonders to explore and enjoy. Like a tourist, I could explore the rich cultures of other people and take away valuable souvenirs. I don't just mean jewelry or other trinkets—though I've had my share. I'm talking about the similarities you find in other cultures, as well as the special and unique differences. This all makes me aware of the beauty of the human experience and reminds me that it's all made possible by such a creative God.

Unfortunately, most people don't understand the true nature of dating. When you tell them you're dating, they automatically assume you're having sex. Maybe that's why I'm different from most people. It's not that I'm not approached or that I'm never tempted. I believe you can control the tone of a relationship all preserving your integrity and keeping it in truth. By not having sex, I haven't missed a thing. In fact, I've taken numerous trips,

Am I Your Enemy Because I Tell You The Truth?

received jewelry, been on luxurious shopping sprees, and received wedding proposals.

Ladies, instead of thinking that all men are dogs, ask yourself what you're doing, saying, and wearing that attracts the ones who are. The reality is that we draw to us what is in us. This does not dismiss the men who have not learned to discipline themselves over their nature.

Which brings me to the thought of those who believe in living together first (put your very heart on lease) is okay. Well let me just say every time you shall have your heart (body, soul, emotions) on lease by staying with your partner you will only lease out what you will pay for, for a lifetime. What's most interesting is that both you and your future mate will generally have to pay for the loss, baggage, disappointments, discouragements, and pain that they did not commit.

It's funny how many double standards exist when it comes to men and women, particularly relating to sex. A woman who has a strong, healthy appetite for sex and has had more than one partner is considered to be loose—some would even call her a hoe. But when a man has a strong, healthy appetite for sex, he is just being a man. In fact, in some cultures his actions are encouraged.

When men don't discipline themselves and work at being faithful, infidelity is inevitable. And don't be fooled into thinking you can change a cheating man. If he was unfaithful before you married him, marriage won't cure him. Enter at your own risk! The only way he can change is, **first, he has to want to change.**

Second, he will need to stay before God, who will be his true accountability partner.

So before you marry someone, be absolutely sure of what you're doing. Long before the wedding day, look for the signs the Lord may be calling your attention to. When you pray and God gives you answers, pay attention to them and be obedient.

I have been privileged to receive several beautiful proposals for marriage from some great men, and not one of them did I take for granted. In fact, I would accept them even before I really knew. I was young and inexperienced and had not yet had my greater rendezvous of truth.

I was blown away by the fact that a man would want to share his life with me and prepare himself with me in mind. It didn't hurt that the rings were always exceptionally amazing, but the greater impact for me was that he chose me. So not only was I honored, but I also felt some sense of obligation to fulfill their wishes as well. That didn't mean that I did not love them, because certainly at those times in my yet-evolving life, I did feel some sort of connection. But I was still learning how to make decisions, especially with matters of the heart.

It has always amazed me how society, our families, as well as people in the church have bought into the idea that every single (one whole number) woman hopes to get married. There's nothing wrong with marriage. God Himself instituted it. But we have been persuaded that a woman is not living unless she has someone.

Am I Your Enemy Because I Tell You The Truth?

I believe that you should be living before he comes so that when he does come you won't require him to give you life. Rather, you will be able to share with him a whole life. I believe whole men are attracted to whole women, but certainly a half a woman plus half a man is a whole mess.

Many of us have made choices because of many lies. We said we had no other choice. We had children to think about, our parents, friends, family, pastors, or priests had to approve of them. They had to be rich. He had to be handsome. She had to be pretty. It's not that those things don't matter, but they shouldn't be the total basis on which a decision is made. God allows us to make our own decisions because He has given us free will, but He will give us signs to guide us in making the important decisions, especially marriage.

When you take someone on your life's journey that you should have left behind, there will always be a cost. From Abraham taking his nephew Lot, Samson seeing Delilah, and Moses taking his brother Aaron, there was a cost. You might get what you want, but ultimately you might not want what you got. Do know a fish and bird can fall in love but where will they live?

Before you trust anyone else, why not first trust the Creator, the King of kings and the Lord or lords? In any relationship, the essence of trust is not in its bind but in its bond.

I had witnessed so many unhealthy marriages that I wasn't in a big hurry to get married. I knew I was still learning myself. My parents and grandparents on both sides of my family had been married all of my life. Though their longevity certainly spoke volumes and is deserving of praise, there were many things that I witnessed that I would not want to bring into my marriage.

This tie was so sensual that because it had no spiritual content or foundation, it was inevitably not going to last. When anything has to rely solely on soullessness, it causes the senses to work overtime to keep it afloat. When something is built on the Spirit and its foundations, it can endure anything, conquer anything, and outlast anything because it is saturated with love.

The thing about senses is that they are constant, and perception is the way we interpret those senses. But most times, we operate with limited perception because of the lie. The more you are exposed to something and the more you experience it, you will discover that your tastes change.

One of my favorite comedians is Eddie Murphy. In his movie *Raw*, he shared a revelation: He compared a person's desire for another person to wanting a particular food. He said that if you are hungry and someone gives you a cracker, you would swear that that cracker was the best one you'd ever tasted. But long after you've eaten a lot of those crackers, and your hunger has been satisfied, the crackers won't seem as special. You'll come to realize that they were just regular old crackers.

It's the same with the way we see other people. You can desire someone so much that when you're first with that person, you think it's the greatest experience in the world. But in time, reality sets in. The newness of the relationship wears off, and the honeymoon

Am I Your Enemy Because I Tell You The Truth?

period is over. Soon, you'll see that person as quite ordinary, and in some cases, you might even find that person no longer desirable at all. But reality only opens our eyes long after we've invested a lot of time and energy in the relationship, spent thousands of dollars on the wedding, made sacrifices in our careers, and children are born.

Once I was engaged to man I thought I loved, but I eventually came to the realization that we weren't right for each other. This realization didn't come from my soul or my mind because my spirit would not allow it. But I realized that the relationship was not the right fit for my spirit. In fact, I often found myself putting more effort into what should have just spiritually flowed. I had tried to break off the relationship even before we were engaged, but I always went back to him and thought it was love.

What proceeds a wedding day is the answer you receive when you pray

Compatibility is the key to a wonderful relationship, not compromise. You cannot always endure what doesn't fit, and why should you? You can't force it to fit.

Although my transformation of the truth was working its course, because I had accepted this engagement, everything was on track to proceed for a beautiful wedding. My fiancé and I had received the approval of our families, and our pastors were in total agreement. The pastors' approval was especially crucial for me at the time because I relied on their word more than anything. I considered them my spiritual parents, and I thought of their sound counseling almost as if it were a voice coming from God Himself.

So everyone was on the bandwagon. My maternal grandmother was going to prepare dinner for the wedding party, and to have her prepare dinner was beyond any five-star dining experience! My finance had arranged for the reception to take place at one of Detroit's finest venues. With all of this pomp, everyone was excited and preparing to make this a beautiful experience–– everyone but me.

My fiancé and my bridesmaid were more excited than any bride would be. So much money was spent and so many invitations were had gone out. Everything seemed to be falling into place, but I was falling apart. Because my identity trumps my plans and the plans of others, what felt like I was falling apart were really those things that had not yet come together, but my destiny would come to pass.

Without going through all the many details my spirit had no rest nor peace. Although this was suppose to be one of the most happiest times of my life I was in encumbered with an unrest. Up into that point it was as if I was carrying an elephant I was so burden down.

I had to suffer the embarrassment and endure the cost/loss and conclude despite everyone else's approval, **God** did not approved. I had to give back his ring and cancel the wedding, the moment I made the decision the burden began to lighten but when I gave his ring back and canceled the wedding I not only immediately felt the

Am I Your Enemy Because I Tell You The Truth?

burden totally remove but I was immediately was catapult unto a heavenly bliss and greater purpose because of the act of obedience.

You have to come this point of revelation. But remember that your spirit led by God's Spirit trumps the plans of others and will guide you to the right someone and place so that you can truly live happily ever after!

Stop Being an Accountant

You ever walked into a room, situation, program, organization for which up into this point, things were well and then unbeknownst to you the unforseen occur. You have been the victim of a lie. You were previously welcomed with open arms, your reputation had proceeded you with nothing less than the best regard. Because of your personality, skills, knowledge, and perseverance and ability to take all things to greater heights you were both well received and approved. The approval of the boss, the pastor, the influential family member, was in place but unbeknownst to you your shine and approval has ruffled feathers of your would- be character assassinators. Regardless how kind you were to them your professionalism, courtesies, compromise, dumbing down, nor humility could not have prepared you for what happens next.

Without your intention of causing any harm of any sort, your only interest is to meet the common goal of interest. Yet, although you did not do anything, besides show-up and give of yourself you did not do or say anything to warrant **this**. Solely because you couldn't be stop with the other tactics, politics, and other nonsense, the final attack is launched ,they have fired off their arsenal of the....LIE. This is the del cume grande!

Their lies can and will be so far fetch from your character that you would even wonder who are they talking about, (I personally believe its just really their own character and all its wiles of insecurities and evil) but it fits for their agenda though it will make for some form of entertainment. Though being very hurtful and certainly disappointing to you this pain was not deserving nor should you receive it.

I recall an incident where I was on a job for over 15 years, after some promotions and such I was placed in a new positions and location.

Little did I know I was yet on the potters wheel to work out His will, that afforded me to grow internally while enduring some major challenges externally on the job. These challenges included but not limited to being gossiped about, lies, a series of harassments, and oftentimes plotted against, yet I continued to do my job with excellence and humbly handled everyone with both professionally and extensive kindness, especially those who deliberately showed me ill-will.

In all my efforts, though sometimes painful I vowed within myself to never let them see me sweat, I waited until I got home to relieve myself.

One day I made it home and ran to my altar (my living room floor) and had that gut busting cry of dealing with the constant backlash. After prayer the Lord first showed me Himself healing and blessing the people in whom sung "Hosanna towards Him', but just a few scriptures later the same people said "cruicfy Him". After a few emotional release He spoked this scripture to me.

Father forgive them: for they know not what they do... Luke 23:34

You must know that people don't often know what they are doing, in fact they have been consumed by their own jealousies and pride being led by the lie, that it's you when in fact it's them.

After going back the next day to the office I shined more of God's glory on them, with a heavier dosage of love. The following week I had even extended to the "main corporal" an invite to one of my prayer fellowships, she came and boy did she have a good time and was released, between all of her tears and yells of victory everyone including her was left with amazement, but not God.

In fact, God will later show me, that had I responded to any of that stuff with retaliation of hate I could have never extended her and invite nor have this great result.

Her soul salvation for eternity and the victory of God's glory on display was far more important than my temporal discomfort. Besides Jesus and other disciples experienced far more challenges; with blood shed, burned in oil, set on fire and whipped to pieces, and I'm complaining of someone talking about me and their unsuccessful plots.

When people hurt us, we go on with our lives, but we never quite let the wounds heal so we can leave it behind. Instead, we keep a running tab of who hurt us, why, and when. Then when we're feeling down, we flip back through our mental account books and tally up all of the hurts, pains, heartbreaks, disappointments, abandonments, arguments, and betrayals.

Are you a necrophiliac?

Are you lending your emotions, body, and time to dead things and situations that have passed already?

If you find yourself keeping track of all the hurts and failures you've endured from others, here's my advice to you: Stop taking a continual account of everyone and everything that has wronged you in some way, large or small. You cannot afford to keep looking back. Remember that you're not here alive and well to go backwards. You are living to go forward. In order to do that, you must learn the lessons of your painful past, but take the lessons with you and leave behind the past and its pain.

Let the dead bury the dead......

You really have to forget those things that are behind and press towards the mark ahead. **Know there is a set place of victory with your name on it,** its positioned for you and waiting for you.

Now it will be unrealistic to continue to use the "forgive and forget", cliche, the pain won't allow you to do that. What I am saying you have to discover what's great ahead to let go what's dead behind this will require what I call the "embrace and let go stroke", this dance requires you to simultaneously release and receive. Take your time you will get the rhythm and the dance, do it to your tune no one else. Remember you are not alone you

Am I Your Enemy Because I Tell You The Truth?

have a great dance partner , Jesus ,knows all the steps and slides, He really invented the dance hustles.

Next time you get in your car, look at the small inscription printed on your side mirror. It says, "Objects in the mirror are closer than they appear." Now think about your past. What happened 25 years ago might still seem big to you, especially if you frequently revisit it and rehash it over and over. But, actually, that 25-year-old hurt is not really as big as it may appear, so leave it alone, and leave it in the past where it belongs. Instead, look ahead because your future is so much closer and better than you can ever imagine.

I'm not telling you that what you've been through didn't hurt or cause serious damage. But even the worst wounds should eventually heal, if allowed to. They may leave scars that stay with you for life, but the scar is your body's way of saying that what used to be here has been healed.

Even Haters Have a Purpose

Believe it or not, your enemies and haters are necessary in your journey, so don't get upset if you find them all along the way. They're there to teach you valuable lessons that you would may not learn from those who love you. You don't even have to worry about destroying your haters. Many times, they will create a fire only later to choke on their own smoke.

I know what I'm talking about. I found haters even within my own family. My mother was often a dream-killer, but since she was more passive-aggressive, I thought of her as a quiet assassin.

Tonya M. Thomas

Though she wouldn't always lead the assault, she would often take it to levels of no return. It's the silent killers who usually hide themselves in the circle or among the lynch mob, wearing a disguise of Christianity but with a heart full of deceit and jealousy.

"A man enemies will be the members of his own household" Matt. 10:36

I thank God continuously for His Word because it has equipped me with great understanding. I think about the stories from the Word of God that help me to understand better what I've gone through in my own experiences. These biblical testimonies have helped me release the desire for vengeance against my haters, and the Scriptures have given me a great sense of comfort, like David and Joseph (for which I have been Josephine-female version of Joseph). My family like Joseph jealousy didn't understand that he was beloved that he could later sustain and preserve their posterity.

I enjoy reading the Book of Esther. Mordechai, Esther's cousin, was a faithful man of God. Haman, who held the highest position in the king's court, plotted Mordechai's downfall. But Haman's plans came to nothing, and, eventually, his jealousy caused him to hang on the same gallows he had built to kill Mordechai.

I'm also inspired by the perennial Christmas favorite *How the Grinch Stole Christmas*. Like me, you might have grown up watching it every year. The lonely, jealous Grinch slinks down from his home on Mount Crumpit late Christmas Eve. He breaks in to each house in the village of Whoville and steals all of the Whos' presents, Christmas decorations, and the food for the great holiday feast.

Am I Your Enemy Because I Tell You The Truth?

Then, from atop his mountain lair, the Grinch looks down at Whoville as the sun comes up Christmas morning, waiting for the sound of the Whos crying and complaining about their ruined Christmas Day. How surprised he was, then, when instead of hearing crying he heard singing as all the Whos gathered in the town square to celebrate the day anyway. What the Grinch didn't know was that the Whos' joy was never in the presents, decorations, and food; it was in the day itself and the love it brought.

That's why many of your haters will be amazed when instead of becoming angry and giving up, you press forward with joy in your heart and a smile on your face. They don't understand that whatever darts they've thrown, whatever shots they've fired, have not stopped your progress because your joy is not in their approval or in anything else they can give you. You're rooted and grounded in Christ, and "the joy of the Lord is your strength" (Nehemiah 8:10).

"I can only be me and you can only be you"!!!

What motivates those who hate you and try to ruin you? I believe the biggest problem is fear. They're afraid of their own past, but they also fear that you might surpass them. They're afraid of what you might become and that whatever you achieve might allow you to outshine them. Never recognizing we all are uniquely made fearfully and wonderfully that no one can beat you being you.

CHAPTER 6
Wherever You Put Your Energy, That's What You Energize

Everything is not worthy of your attention or your most valuable commodity: time.

One of the mistakes we make is expending our energy in the wrong places, but we also don't look beyond the surface to find out what's really going on. I advise you to take your energy, and look beyond. Preserve your energy, and don't give it to anyone who does not deserve it.

Where Do You Put Your Energy?
We often hear people talk about "the rat race," the seemingly unending quest to keep up with the fast pace of life. That includes pursuing education and careers, making time for our families and leisure activities, amassing more money and material things, and meeting and connecting with the right people. In all this activity, where are we putting our energy?

Wherever you're putting your energy is where you're spending most of your time. But the question you have to ask yourself is, Is it worth it? Despite all of our busyness, despite all the energy we expend to make things happen, we might still end up unfulfilled and empty, our lives a vast void still needing to be filled.

Perhaps we need to shift our focus from the things we usually pursue and examine the things we have put on the back burner or left unattended. For many of us, the first thing we shove into the background is the spiritual aspect of our lives. While we work countless hours each week, spend time working out our bodies, and then feel entitled to pursue leisure activities, we often crowd out the most important person in our lives: God.

But God is there for us when our supervisors, spouses, friends, siblings, children, and networking acquaintances can't, or won't, be. We invest much energy and time pursuing success, wealth, and health, and there's nothing wrong with any of those things. But when they pull us completely away from our Creator and cause us to lose focus on what's really important, then they are not to our benefit but to our detriment.

When God created us, He created us with a God-sized void that only He can fill. Although we do our best to fill that void with more hours at work, more hours in the gym, extreme sports, alcohol, drugs, sex, shopping, cars, money, houses, relationships, and any other human pursuit, we are only wasting our time. God wants us to allow His Spirit to reign in our lives and to occupy that space so that we may be "complete in him" (Colossians 2:10).

God knows that wherever we spend most of our energy, that's what's going take up most of our time. Instead, He wants us to invest in Him because the returns are immeasurable! Matthew says, "Lay up for yourselves treasures in heaven, where neither moth nor rust doth corrupt, and where thieves do not break through and steal: *For where your treasure is, there will your heart be also*" (Matthew 6:20-21, emphasis added).

Stop putting your energy into things/people/programs/institutions that don't yield back something to you. You may not ever control who is in the Whitehouse, school house, or jail house but you can control what goes on in your house. So use your valuable energy to first built your house up and yield the fruits thereof.

Compromise Is Deceitful

The enemy is good at deceiving us into believing that we can compromise our way to something better, something that will empower us and boost our self-esteem. So we invest a lot of time and energy thinking up our plans and how best to compromise so that it benefits us the most, only to find that we've come up empty.

I used to work a night job where I had constant run-ins with my supervisor. He was arrogant and rude and expected everyone to bow to him or risk his wrath. But I wasn't born to bow to anyone but the Lord, so I didn't let him break me, even when he shot his best shot.

Whenever I would not comply to my supervisors methods of harassments, I could always count on him to give me the worst work assignments or to cut my lunch break simply because he could. But I wasn't the only co-worker who was singled out. That co-worker, unlike me, received special treatment. The supervisor allowed her to work overtime when she wanted to, gave her less work that was easier to do, and never challenged her when she wanted to take time off. But all of this latitude came with a price.

My co-worker had compromised herself in order to win the approval of our supervisor, who would make lewd comments about her body and even touch her inappropriately. The more she accepted his advances the worse it got, and the other employees took liberties with her as well. But it finally reached a boiling point.

One day, the supervisor called out my co-worker. Everyone gathered around. Then the supervisor compared her to a stripper and suggested that she entertain us. The guys in the crowd cheered her on. I could tell she was embarrassed, but she joined in to hide her pain. But this was more than I could take. I spoke up in my coworker's defense, although she hadn't asked me to, and that's all my supervisor needed to hear. I had embarrassed him in front of everyone, and he wasn't going to let that go unaddressed. True to form, he cut my lunch break and gave me a tougher job to do. But it was worth it for what happened next.

Later that night, my co-worker came to me and asked, "Why did you stick up for me? You know the supervisor doesn't like you." I told her that she was right. The supervisor didn't like me, but I told her that he didn't like her, either. The look of shock on her face said it all. She had gotten so caught up in the special attention, the groping, the catcalls, and the lewd comments that she had no clue that she wasn't liked. Her compromise had bought her a few favors, but it didn't make her well liked at all.

Am I Your Enemy Because I Tell You The Truth?

Many people buy into the lie of compromise. Their ambition and ego tell them that they should get where they want to go by whatever means necessary, but compromise will cost you more than you're willing to pay and can afford.

My co-worker thought that by letting our supervisor and the other coworkers debase her that her stock was rising. Just because the supervisor was throwing a few favors her way made her think she was going somewhere. But she was wrong. On the other hand, I was treated like a criminal and given the worse jobs, but God gave me favor, which was greater than anything our supervisor could have given me.

In fact, not only was I able to be a light to many of the people who worked in that department, but I was blessed to be able to lead my co-worker to the Lord. Many of the people I worked with accepted Christ and later became contributors to my ministry and community center—all because I took a stand and didn't compromise.

During that time of testing, I often wondered if God saw what was happening. I wondered if He heard my prayers and saw my tears. Many times, I felt like the children of Israel must have felt working for a taskmaster like Pharaoh who forced them to make brick without straw. But I needn't have worried. God was working on me, through me, and for me.

In God's timing, the supervisor lost his position and went through a divorce, but I was offered another position with more pay and better benefits. The position was so good that I no longer had to work two jobs. That experience taught me that compromising doesn't pay off, and even when I feel alone, God will always give me the victory.

Who tells the Lion story.............?
As aforementioned in my childhood being a parentifed child had its role in shaping my views and posture, enabling me to form and practiced certain methodologies. But my core of passion and what would strike and provoke response and attention from me was what I was simply born with.

I imagine having a conversation with a lion who is instinctively known for his fierce and strategic response of courage as he his yet territorial of his claim of what he deems as what is important to him. His instinctive nature is both understood and respected by others that he is regarded and held to a regard of nothing less than his claim/purpose for which he was built, courageous.

> The lion has always been known first and foremost of his appearance and attributes, before he can even roar to you his name and his inner thoughts. His presence and natural attributes take on a conversation of themselves and are felt to all that are in his presence. The lion attributes of being strong, fierce, courageous, protective, aggressive, brave, willing to fight, hunter, group members (part of a pride), and loners in the big scheme of things.

Am I Your Enemy Because I Tell You The Truth?

He is the king of the jungle because he if first king within, the elaborate way of his conveying his will both by his posture and his stands has made his mark permanent, his footprint sketch, his legacy unpolished, and his name unchangeable. It is what solidifies him and his purpose when he his able to walk in it a stand in himself, even when he is developing.

You see like the lion sometimes your roar, presence, legacy, talents and gifts, appearance can proceed before others it is these things that carry a conversation on their own, that often times have many with an expected perception that you "have and must" live up to, so they say.

The truth of the matter is Lions don't **always** roar, sometimes they cry sometimes their scared, tired, and sometimes their loneliness bleeds them to pain unknown.

So oftentimes people who have always played the hero, the encourager, the fixer, the healer, fought for, stood for, provided for, stood in the prayer gap for, risk their life for, took a bid for, sacrifice money and time for, stayed for…more than often have not anyone to do the same for them.

How many times has you seen a gazelle, giraffe, or an elephant look out for a lion? But in many instance a lion presents has preserved and protected even those animal even from becoming preys to the hyenas.

What is so amazing about you is that you give well to others more often than yourself. You are also always more critical of yourself, because even you don't give yourself a space for error or chance and you already know your haters won't, that why I say; Never judge a person by one weak point in their life. It's amazing you could have done a 100 things right, and right at the brink of discouragement, worried, fearfulness, grief, depression, you make a decision. And all the naysayers would like to call you out.

What is most unfortunate is that your needs often never shows up on anyone's radar, though you walk alone, fight alone, give alone, cry alone, and worry alone, ...you are **never alone**.

You, like a lion, like a giraffe were made with hearts, that though everyone has one it's proportion to accommodate the built of each. The weight of a giraffe heart is about 25 pounds and his lungs can hold about 12 gallons of air. The giraffe's heart is so big because it has to be big and strong enough to pump the blood in his body. Like you maybe you have a big heart because like the giraffe your neck and head can see where a lot of others can't see. Remember the turtle and the giraffe will always have a different conversation about what they see, while both can stretch their necks they both will see different things according to their abilities.

The turtle can tell you about the grass and some few plants and the giraffe tell you more about the top of trees and the skies, neither one is lying they are speaking from their respected capacity. The truth is we were all build according to His plan and purpose and are equipped for it.

You must know the truth that you were uniquely build and wire to only get your specific needs (emptiness, total fulfillment, and understanding, by the King of king, the" Lion of Judah"

Am I Your Enemy Because I Tell You The Truth?

Now I know you might say Ms. Tonya "sometimes I just need someone of flesh to talk to vent, to simply just share with immediately.

Let me finish before you count this out. (geez), believe me I totally feel you. Like Jesus you would often see him have the "three" to whom he will go a distant with Peter, James and John, because they **can go** the distant with him. These eagles as you will soon discover if you allow are few even in your life. Maybe if you really get still and take inventory of your life, maybe just maybe you have too many chickens in your life and are not embracing, acknowledging, or welcoming the eagles in your life. Too many times you give way to your fleshy/carnal way of choosing and by popular demand you choose people and give those individual's titles that they are neither fit for or deserve. Never mistake longevity, or I knew you when, or we go way back as a means to determine who should be in your friend zone. After all chickens/ and chicken heads and eagles all have wings, but their ability to fly are altogether different. The chicken bodies are big and their wings are small, they are ground feeder, they can't fly high and when they do they can only go a short distance. Like some people in your life they have big talk, big dreams about you and them but they are not flying anywhere, their big bodies/talk exceed the wingspan (capacity) that all they can give/offer you is a lot of talk.

Their ground feeders they feed off the ground/low way of thinking, the daily gossip, lies and deceits. They feed off of others abilities, because all the can get and contain are the left-overs, they are always doing and eating "the same Ole same ole"- a different day same chicken.

But the Eagle, his wings span goes beyond his body and weight in fact it is known that eagles wing span (capacity of life) is longer and larger than his body everything he **does is big**. The eagle's seven foot-wing span allows it to glide effortlessly at altitudes of over 2,400 feet, thus giving the illusion that the eagle is moving slow, like you, you are moving so fast and accomplishing so much but to the average/chicken you may appear to be slow, (slow of telling them off-even when you know there not worth two dead flies, slow to anger and wrath, which is only meekness/controlled anger on display but, not always showing your hand or having instant gratification by way of substandard tools (large cars and homes, affluence and notoriety, yet always making strides on so many heights that they can see how high you are because there too low to come up anyway, in fact if you were to invite them you will have to carry them up to your nest to begin with. The eagle is capable of carrying objects which larger than its own body weight, the eagles have been known to transport small lambs a distance of several miles.

Because the eagle's wings/feathers are so special they have separation in their feathers at the tips like fingers of a hand. These separations play a major role in the power and stability of **the eagle in flight**.

Like you even when they call you "anti-social, weird, unfriendly, bougie, "think you better than," the truth of the matter is first;

Am I Your Enemy Because I Tell You The Truth?

Jesus went a stone-cast away from his boys-to get adjusted for his next/new level. Separation is essential for you not only to get up but to stay up. Having the ability to get away from low thinking/ground feeders all their sources comes from low living and low having and if not careful you can get some of their stuff on you, you must know its hard being big when little got a hold of you.

The eagle's vision is exceptionally sharp because each yet has two "fovea" (areas of acute vision), as compared to with the human eye, which has only one. The eagle's fovea are very small and tightly grouped allowing the eagle to see small details from extremes distances. For example, an eagle can spot an object as small as a rabbit from a distance of almost 2 miles! A man (ordinary-without God) would have to have a pair of powerful binoculars to see the same thing. You have to limit your group to a tight-few for the next dimension of your journey in life and make sure that your group is tight;-the group may only entail you –your mate-your child, or sometimes me-myself-and I.

When that group becomes tightly fit with our Lord and Savior Jesus Christ, than does the vision become. You will be able first to see yourself correctly and truthful and be able to see the lie (people, the hidden agendas, the game, the set ups, "the oaky dokes", their declaration of love or the lack thereof, perpetual fears) miles ahead, ridding yourself of all the nonsense and foolishness that it came to bring.

Each year the eagle replaces its feathers over a period of several months. However, unlike other birds/chickens/people, the eagle is not severely handicapped during his "shedding time". The eagle is still able to continue hunting throughout the entire renewal process.

This is why the solitude is necessary that you will swiftly see what you need and don't need in your life. This shedding will include but not limited to the shedding of old habits, people, practices, mind sets, methodologies, old church, old friends, another job, another position, old lovers, eating habits, sleeping habits-alone and otherwise, certain types of entertainment and spending habits, just to name a few.

You will not die in these moments always instantly, in fact, while most people will bend over, bow over , just die over even the very idea of not holding on to some of these things or people, the eagle would just …continue even through the process. The process can and will be painful, hurtful, and even lonely but guess what…you will live and continue to fly high.

Some times like the lion, hero , and the eagle us is oftentimes ostracized, shot at with lies and gossip, poison by the jealous, trap by the seducer, molested by the media, wounded by love ones, trapped by the system, pursued for the kill. But baby there is a law/God in place they will soon be cut down, don't you dare fret, because it really is a terrible thing to fall in the hands of the living God and angry God when you touch or mishandle "His chosen".

Am I Your Enemy Because I Tell You The Truth?

"In my distress [when seemingly closed in] I called upon the Lord and cried to my God; He heard my voice out of His temple (heavenly dwelling place), and my cry came before Him, into His [very] ears. Then the earth quaked and rocked, the foundations also of the mountains trembled; they moved and were shaken because He was indignant and angry." There went up smoke from His nostrils; and lightning out of His mouth devoured; coals were kindled by it. He bowed the heavens also and came down; and thick darkness was under His feet. And He rode upon a cherub [a storm] and flew [swiftly]; yes, He sped on with the wings of the wind. (AMPC)

My friends warn your enemies and their comrades (being the cowards that they are, they are never alone-they need a group); the naysayers, the ex's, the family members, the coworkers, the bosses, the judges, the loan officers, probation officers, the guards, the polices, the teachers, the unhealthy family members, the unhealthy parents, the neighbors, the baby's mommas, the baby daddies, the went not sent Pastors, the coaches, that they don't even have a fighting chance messing with you.

Yes, hero/shero/Lion/Lioness/Eagle you do have a place to go share your story; get among like- minded pray and ask God to help you choose so that you won't lose.

In closing my eagle/comrade/Lion what will always give you your distinction will be your ability of keeping "the main thing", "the main thing" there's is coming very soon a true gathering of all eagles where we all should be striving for, the gathering for the coming of our Lord and Savior Jesus Christ.

"For as the lighting comes from the east and flashes to the west, so also will the coming of the Son of Man be. For wherever the carcass is, there the eagles will be gathered. Matthew 24:27-28.

The understanding of this scripture is this; the location of a carcass is visible from great distances because of the circling of birds' carrion birds overhead. Similarly, Christ's return will be clearly evident to all near and far. The same point is made by the lightning. The eagle-carcass imagery here also speaks of the judgment that will accompany His return.

Let's gather and be ready!!!!!!

CHAPTER 7
Places of Worship: Lifelines or Shipwrecks?

Religious institutions have suffered brutally for standing for the truth.

What Is Going On?

The Book of Acts details how the early church suffered persecution. People met secretly in order to worship. Even today, there are places around the world where God's people aren't allowed to worship freely. They meet in clandestine places and smuggle Bibles into their country. If caught, they face imprisonment and sometimes death. I am most grateful, yet oftentimes I myself have taken for granted that I am in a country that I can pick my bible up at my leisure, watch an expose myself to great teaching of God's incredible word. I can go into a church, my home, a local park and lift up my holy hands and give God an incredible praise.

But many of us take church for granted. It's just another thing to check off our long to-do list each week. If we miss a service, we shrug it off nonchalantly. We promise God we'll make it up to Him next week.

Because of our lax attitude toward God and the things of God, our churches have grown lazy. Our worship has gone stale. Many churches operate on autopilot whether the Spirit shows up or not. In many ways, they are asleep with their eyes wide open.

In my hometown of Detroit, there are more churches than there are schools , healthy neighborhoods,or job-training sites, or jobs with competitive wages. Yet despite the profusion of churches, the community is still sick, and the neighborhood houses are crumbling. In a one-mile radius, or on every block, there are at least five churches or more; and lined up alongside the churches are liquor stores, beauty stores, hair salons, and fast-food joints. So people in the community might look good on the outside and satisfy their natural hunger, but they're empty on the inside.

Many churches have grown indifferent to the move of the Spirit. They're more interested in appearances than transformation. The apostle Paul warned of those who are not walking in the Spirit: They have "a form of godliness, but [are] denying the power thereof" (2 Timothy 3:5). Instead of operating in the Spirit to discern what hungry souls need, many pastors are satisfied preaching people happy and not preaching them free. In fact most are concerned with quantity of people they have then to assist and build a quality people.

It All Starts With Leaders

I personally have witnesses some of this World greatest spiritual leaders. People like Bishop TD Jakes, Oral Roberts, George Bogel, Bishop Gilbert Patterson, Jackie McCullough, Bishop Paul Morton, Noel Jones, Pastor Chris Brooks, Pastor Keith Vincent,

Am I Your Enemy Because I Tell You The Truth?

Joyce Meyers, Bishop David Ellis I. These spiritual Giants have helped shaped this world to so many dimensions untold.

Bishop David Ellis I was one of the first leader that displayed kingdom in its most purest form. He not only founded and led a church but he opened and ran schools, housing for low income families, senior citizen homes, and my favorite "a credit union". This great man of "God' for me truly **got it**, what I would call a healthy balanced church.

Although he had many members he was such a giant of God's love that you will literally in his presence be touched by the love of God. Bishop Ellis ministry would be felt and embraced by the communities, government, and other ministries. I personally believe because of first his huge heart and relationship with God along with his beautiful wife, he allowed the seed in him to germinate not only in his respected church location that he impacted the entire city of Detroit, Michigan. There is not a person, churched or unlearned, police or criminal, gang member or student, that lives in Detroit, Michigan who have not heard or been embraced by his seeds.

God is not pleased with spiritual leaders who do not carry out His assignment to effectively lead His people. Read the stories of people such as King Saul and Eli the priest. God places great responsibility on spiritual leaders, and He expects them to be first-partakers and good examples before His people.

Unfortunately, many problems in church start in the pulpit. Pastors stand firm in those areas they themselves have overcome, but they tiptoe around the areas they have not overcome. So they set the tone for the congregation to call out a Top 10 list of sins that are an abomination to them, but any other sins, especially the sins of the heart—such as lying, envy, anger, jealousies, unforgiveness, and pride are often given a pass. They would literally place hierarchical towards sin and its practice. Oftentimes this is the case for those would-be leaders who have those struggles in those areas, that they will show more grace for the areas they struggle most in and not the others. So fornication, adultery, lying, and back-biting would get a past. All while homosexuals, drug abusers, and murders would get the death penalty of hell fire and brimstone. When all have sinned and short.

Please know I don't have a problem with pastors doing well financially, but I believe that as leaders, pastors should help raise their congregations spiritually, mentally, and financially to be their neighbors. Paul said we are joint-heirs with Christ (Romans 8:16-17). He also said God is no respecter of persons, which means we stand equally before our Creator. We are of one body: "For by one Spirit are we all baptized into one body, whether we be Jews or Gentiles, whether we be bond or free; and have been all made to drink into one Spirit" (1 Corinthians 12:13).

What I am bothered by is church members not being concerned about those in the community who are hurting, suffering, and dying. Our children are going to failing schools, teens are getting in trouble, drug use is on the rise, and families are being ripped apart.

Am I Your Enemy Because I Tell You The Truth?

Meanwhile, churches are having incredible high emotional services while their own homes, communities, and surrounding areas are suffering.

How can any church ignore the plight of its community and not do anything to reach out and help those around them? God-called and Spirit-led churches should be taking over their communities for the Kingdom and working to restore righteousness. Real churches are not effecting their church internally but externally as well, even governmentally, isn't that what Jesus did?

Some people grow up in abusive households and then enter other abusive relationships or engage in self-afflicted abuse. With a history of abuse, sometimes they are drawn to abusive churches. In the very place where they ought to receive love and compassion, they often face judgment, punishment, and an absence of truth about God's plans for their lives. One of the reasons for church abuse can be found in leadership. First off, stop limiting abuse with an understanding of physical abuse only. The greater part of abuse is mental the abuse or misuse of any individual is beyond devastation.

Many of the men and women who lead God's people are themselves slaves to sin and condemnation. As slaves, they preach and disciple others who then become slaves, therefore reproducing and perpetuating the cycle of sin and bondage.

Instead of teaching and preaching the gospel, these leaders reinforce hurt, pain, and sin. Because they haven't been healed and set free, they continue the lineage of slavery with God's people.

That's not to say that God didn't call these leaders. They may well have a mighty anointing on their lives. Although the anointing breaks the yoke, they are not operating in the anointing God has given them and are working in their own flesh.

One warning sign you might find in church is when leadership has lost focus on God and the things of God and places more emphasis on money. The most important focus of any body of believers is God's Word, followed by worship and praise. If these are a church's priority, then everything else will align in its proper place.

While sacrificial giving of one's material substance is biblical and right for each person to do, it's not the most important thing God requires. God **loves** and **desires us.** He wants us to sacrifice ourselves in worship and praise and in putting aside those things that separate us from Him. When we give of ourselves, we please and glorify Him.

Another pitfall in church is when members jockey for position and power. If position is the only reason you go to church, examine your spirit. Ask God to return you to your first love––Him (Revelation 2:4).

Some leaders also are more interested in how many people fill the pews than in how many of those people walk out of the sanctuary saved and victorious. God can work with countless millions of people, or He can work with one person––and all numbers in between.

Am I Your Enemy Because I Tell You The Truth?

Though we are ambassadors for Christ, and our mission is to harvest as many souls for the Kingdom as we can, God never placed a number on how many. He doesn't reward a pastor for having thousands of members and punish the pastor with only 25 members. I must say that I humbly give much respect to those leaders who were both called and practiced the principles of God. It is not and easy task dealing with "people", dealing with yourself is enough already. I totally commend you for taking on the services, and I will tell everyone you should the same, love, honor, and respect those in leadership for they do deserve it. My position for this part of the book is to remind all spiritual leaders what God is most concerned about, that the pastor is preaching truth and equipping people to live a victorious life.

God's First Lady-the Church

While attending and serving in my first church home I saw and witnessed how God felt about His first lady and how she is treated. Lets just say He always respond.....

Like a jealous husband you don't want to cause harm to His woman (church), for He would fight for her.

The woman, first lady, pastor wife, for a church is paramount. Like a home a healthy home, you will most often be able to contribute that towards the woman of the house or the lack thereof. My former first lady though very wise, beautiful, and incredibly gifted, failed to get and obtain deliverance, discipline and overcome some strongholds in her life.

Tonya M. Thomas

Remember it's always the small foxes that spoil the vine. A beautiful ministry had to suffer at great losses. This amazing ministry was budding in new dimensions that God had ordained for the building of both the ministry and the actual church building. Like Achan ,sin was in the camp and victory was sabotage. At a brink where a church was being built with all members aboard and giving out their needs and wants, some folks had sowed their entire paychecks, their utility bills, emergency cash, went without, gave when it hurt; They were even other measures of asking their family and friends, along with creative building fund efforts that it even went beyond chicken dinners sales, but even collecting pennies, humbly asking the community and surrounding entities to donate. Concerts, an array of talent of congregational members were exercised to meet the goals of this building completion. Victory was sabotage. At a brink where a church was being built with all members aboard and giving out their needs and wants, some folks had sowed their entire paychecks, their utility bills, emergency cash, went without, gave when it hurt; They were even other measures of asking their family and friends, along with creative building fund efforts that it even went beyond chicken dinners sales, but even collecting pennies, humbly asking the community and surrounding entities to donate, concerts, an array of talent of congregational members were exercised to meet the goals of this building completion.

Unfortunately while all this was going on and moving forward at record breaking accounts, there was a major decay going in its foundation. Now do know this building certainly from the architecture and plans looked to be the most beautiful building by its structure, but you must remember that Jesus was the carpenter son, and like the Master that He is, and every skilled builder will tell you that what is priority in building is not its features but rather its foundation.

While all the evident of dysfunction was rising in this ministry from particularly the first lady from gossiping, usurping her authority of the Pastor, jealousies and insecurities began to rule her heart As Saul, though she was called she was in sin and pride contaminated as the heart of her the ministry began to shape itself of that same heart (foundation). All while all of this exceptional monies and support was coming in by the droves to the ministry and the moving on of building was in way there came a sudden stop. It was reported that the grounds for which the church was to be built upon was sitting on some contaminated soil that had prevent the laying of the foundation.

This very costly delay; had to first have a high ticket of having it removed and later place somewhere, this of course was not in the budget, therefore it caused major delay but even the more it cost everyone who was involved towards the building of the new church and the building of their lives/families and those to come.

For a side-note our God is loving that He will always send a warning, but it's up to us to realize that and humble ourselves repent and move forward, this was the only difference between Saul and David, morally speaking David was far less moral than

Saul yet he had true and pure heart to humble himself and seek God's grace and righteousness not his own.

This woman of God would not do that as a result not only were a great deal of monies was lost, but these major delays kept the growth and victory that this church was heading to, many people lives were cut short and growth stunt because like that natural body it's the internal things that go unchecked that later can be both detrimental to the health of an individual, but the growth and functionality of that body can withered and loose its members.

> *Ye did run well; who did hinder you that ye should obey the truth? Galatains 5:7*

While there are women that have mishandle their roles in such positions there are those who handle it well with the love of God, grace, and so much class that their fruit bear witness of them and it yet remains. I think about this beautiful gem of a first lady, her name was Lady Diane Greer-Walker, she was the first lady of Mount Zion Church of Nashville.

Please note also that this generation at this time were the benefactors as all church leader are from who went before them, the position should always be to humbly and graciously take their call and continue to greater heights in love and righteousness, realizing at all times that Jesus Christ is the chief corner stone.

This beautiful humble shell first, kept her relationship with Christ in great order that she in turn was able to function in the proper order with her husband the great Bishop Joseph Walker. Her spirit will exude because she was so engulfed in the Lord and what pleased him. That because of her obedience several churches was built in record breaking time and paid off, ministries were effectively develop, and member to members grew in record breaking numbers.

Although this Angel of light is no longer with us in the natural her fruit has yet stand and attest of her marvelous contributions. This great gift to the Kingdom body of Christ has kept on giving even while she the giver is gone.

Mt. Zion stepping into its existence of 150 yrs., maintaining on founded principles of God's word and love as it's main source.

I know the ancestors are proud of this gem who took the reign and kept the principles as the main thing and kept the "main thing"

My Testimony

As believers, we sometimes become discouraged in church. Sometimes our leaders let us down. Other times, we lose focus and let ourselves down. Here's my personal testimony.

Years ago, I attended a church where I served faithfully.

I respected the church's leadership and sought to do God's will. Because of the wonderful teaching and practiced principles by the leadership, and my thirst for God I grew in Christ by leaps and bounds, and my labor of services of love yielded much fruit until things went horribly wrong.

Like many church members, I thought of my leaders as parents. The thought was further reinforced even by the titles for which they had "Mother, Pastor/Covering. I viewed the church as my family and that's not the problem. Coming from a dysfunctional family and not having parents who nurtured and cared for me as they should have, I was looking for someone in authority to fill that role; and for me, that became the church leaders. I soon learned that was a grave mistake.

I write not these things to shame you, but as my beloved sons I warn you. For though ye have ten thousand instructors in Christ, yet have ye not many fathers: for in Christ Jesus I have begotten you through the gospel 1Corinthians 4:14-15

Because of great teaching of this church I took into practice of the teaching and began my personal journey with the Lord. I began to study further, fast when the church did not fast, and ultimately began and had, through the grace of God a personal relationship.

With a personal relationship with God not church I went to unfounded heights and personal deliverances later leading me to my purpose that **HE ordained**.

One of the many ministries that I learned was in me and birthed was the ministry Children of the King (COK). This ministry was a holistic community service movement, with the sole purpose of taking God's message to everyone from the homeless, to the elite, we provided vocational training, fed the homeless.

Am I Your Enemy Because I Tell You The Truth?

We also started new and effective programs, including a men's group, a liturgical dance ministry, and a drama group. From these groups other ministries were birthed. Even our pastor benefited from these ministries. He was able to widen his circle of influence, especially through the men's group, and was able to reach beyond our church's walls and minister to others.

We did not limit our serving of heartfelt touch of love to the church walls nor a particular race, religion, or creed.

The Lord showed me that He was God and King to all man and forever reigned, and **we were all His children.**

Children of the King, had a wide range of supporters and benefactors. Our supporters included but not limited to Christians, Baptist, Jews, Muslims, Jehovah Witness, Atheist, Arabic, African Americans, Europeans, Latino, Married, Singles, Homosexuals, many different churches all over the city of Detroit and surrounding areas.

Tonya M. Thomas

We had covered so many territories with effective programs, events, crusades,and seminars; that we were recognize and given many awards that included but not limited to "Testimonial Resolutions from the city Council members", Community activist award from the Police, Effective Change and acknowledgment from The Governor of Michigan, we were featured in our City's newspapers and interviews both by radio and television. To God be all the glory!!!

Am I Your Enemy Because I Tell You The Truth?

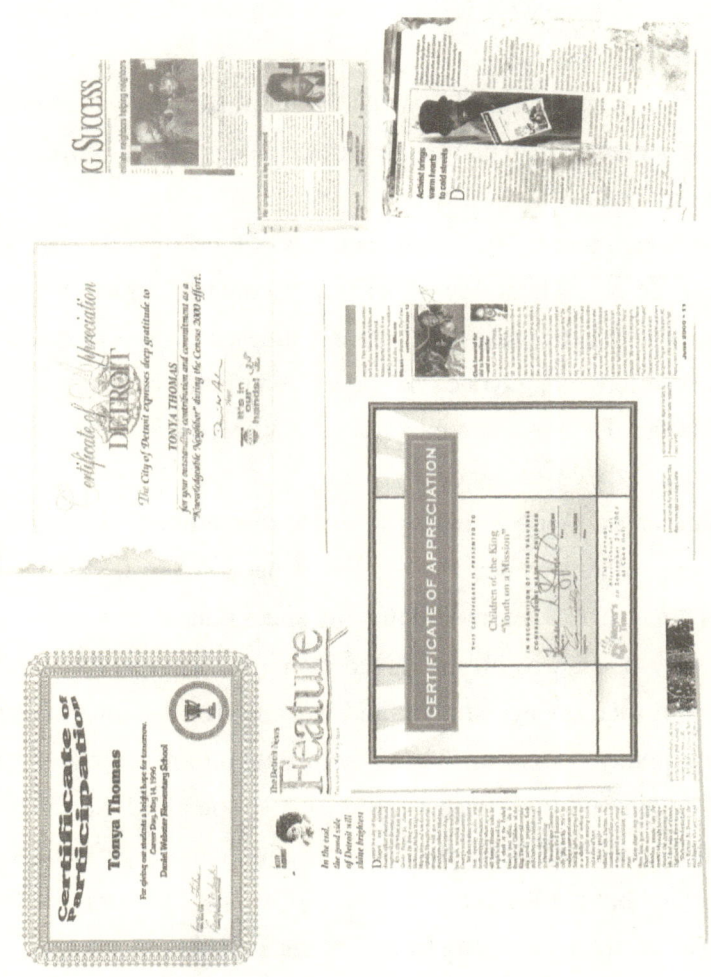

My objective for the ministry never changed and because of the pureness of God's love through me and my son Calvin, He did any and all changes as He saw fit to the people. We humbly knew at all times that we were just His vessels for use. He is the King and we are His children.

Through my relationship with Christ I immediately learned that He was greater than church nor could He be defined or limited to man-made laws and doctrines.

Although there were great teachings of God's word there, there was a lot of mishandling of scriptures context; "to women never wearing pants or make-up, nor preaching with braids in their hair, to not embracing anyone who doesn't share the same doctrine"

Though I believe my pastors were sincere I learned in many instances they were sincerely wrong.

The church with already the majority members coming from poverty, there was not a strong list of people who were educated and upper-class thereby in some instances education was not only priority but it was almost given over like a curse. My already being a then college student and working for the state succumb me to many compromising of both thought and practices when I soon learned that I was a minority. My son and I was also one of the strongest tithers, even with the church many "offerings that included but not limited to church anniversary, pastors birthdays, Christ Birthday, building funds" though I had both mortgage, my sons private school and car notes.

When my son and I joined the church, we opened our hearts as well as our wallets we weren't rich by any means, but we gave of what we had.

Am I Your Enemy Because I Tell You The Truth?

Calvin and I gave money, but we also gave clothes, school supplies, church supplies, and other things that were needed. We gave so much that other members thought the church leaders were the ones behind the gifts. My son and I didn't mind that people didn't know we were responsible for the gifts. God had blessed us with great favor, and we were able to have open doors through which the abundance flowed. Our only concern was that we were in God's will that we were being effective for the Kingdom, and that people's needs were being met.

More importantly, though, Calvin and I were able to bring in souls for the Kingdom. On any given Sunday, there were many people who came to church with us, who gave their lives to Christ, and who were set free and delivered. We didn't pick and choose who we invited. We followed the leading of the Lord and reached out to anyone who was hungry for God, all races, ages, and gender.

In the meantime, as we gave lovingly and sacrificially so God's house might be filled, often, our personal needs were unmet. Many members of the church thought I was rich and that my son and I needed nothing. That wasn't the case at all. God blessed us as we gave out of what He had given us, but we weren't rich, at least my man standards, we were simply rich in faith and engulfed with God's love. Many times we did without so we could give to the house of God.

Calvin and I weren't looking for public recognition or to be paid for what we did. But like a child seeking her parents' approval, the only expectation I had from my leaders was a nod of personal recognition or simply "I'm proud of you."

Instead, I had a David experience. After David returned from killing Goliath, the women sang, "Saul hath slain his thousands, and David his ten thousands" (1 Samuel 18:7). Hearing the people praise David so highly caused King Saul to become jealous. He said, "They have ascribed unto David ten thousands, and to me they have ascribed but thousands: and what can he have more but the kingdom?" (verse 8). Though David had acted heroically when even Saul's own men wouldn't fight the giant, from that point on, the king allowed his anger and jealousy to ruin his relationship with David.

But just as Saul didn't want David to outshine him, our co-pastor saw the fruit my son and I produced but dismissed the cost we had paid for such recognition. What the leaders of our church didn't see was that my son and I fasted when they had not called a church-wide fast. Calvin sacrificed sports and other recreational time to prepare meals for people or to prepare our house so others could come and pray. We transported other members to church, although it was out of our way to do so.

We received support from companies like Ford, US Postal, BCBS, Deluxe Grocers, and a host of local stores and people, but every door we went to was not opened to us. However, the Lord touched the hearts of many people, and many of the doors we knocked on were opened. All of our support came from outside of the church, so most people didn't know where our help came from.

Am I Your Enemy Because I Tell You The Truth?

The Lord had also blessed us with creative fundraisers; We had a many first-timers, we were the first to have what I called "Cruisin With Jesus", we would rent riverboats and cruise the skylines of Detroit and Canada with fine dining and Christian entertainments, We have given concerts and programs with Grammy-winner artists, and we would collaborate with other major businesses for funding purpose.

Even though I could never get the respect of our co-pastor, I continued to love her and treat her as a mother. But like Saul did to David, she targeted me with attacks along with having her would-be committee join her. Once, I went to her to try to resolve our differences. Instead of embracing me in love, she told me she was angry because I had gotten money from companies under the auspices of our church but had not given any of the money to the church.

What she didn't seem to understand was that I had been given the money for my ministry, Children of the King, and I had generously shared of the abundance with the church. That's how Calvin and I were able to give so much. What she also though was purchase with money was not, we actually had more in-kind donations than money.

I was hurt by her words. As much as we had shared with our church and as many people as had benefited from our gifts, including our co-pastor, she had attacked me with harsh words and an unwillingness to understand what had happened. Because of my taking on David's strategies as well as relating to his pain and disappointment, I did not curse God's anointed.

...The prey taken from the mighty, For I will contend with him who contend with you. Isiah 49:25-26.

I learned even through the tears and heartaches that you really have to pray for people who prey on you, because the really don't know what they are doing.

Although this woman had those shameful acts rooted in nothing less than insecurities, fears, and desired control she was still like Saul, chosen. This is where you have to first still honor your leaders regardless of their errors they are leaders, like our natural parent who don't always get it right, or civil leaders, they are yet in authority we have to be mature and responsible of being obedient to God's word and honor them, and simply take it all to God in prayer and watch Him move.

That strategy and ultimate answer of just taking it to God in prayer yield its fruit as well. That same co-pastor and I through the love of God and His turning things around, came back together apologizes were expressed and shared and the relationship was restored even better than before. The church was built and their community interest has grown beyond heights. Truth really did come to the rescue.

Am I Your Enemy Because I Tell You The Truth?

Free people....Free people
We as a people have more in common than not.

> *...From whom the whole body fitly joined together and compacted by that which every joint supplieth, according to the effectual working in the measure of every part, maketh increase of the body unto edification of itself in love. Ephesian 4:16*

People will not give the advantage of your freedom when they have benefited from the advantage of your entrapment.

Freedom is not free at all real freedom will cost you everything.

The cost of being free comes at a grave cost, ask our Father the Lord Jesus Christ.

What He would tell you that you were worth the sacrifice. God's messengers must first internalize God's truth for himself, then preach (proclaim) it to others and know that God does not always call the qualified but he does always qualify the called. While preaching certainly proclaims, teaching explains what is most powerful for people is understanding.

Information that is understood can be practiced is more powerful than an emotional sensational mood that can later fade away, until the next power of persuasion. With great teaching, one can walk away grounded with resolute for permanent change.

Tonya M. Thomas

Where Does That Leave God's People?

"I don't steal sheep, I grow grass"------Bishop Joseph Walker

One of the most important decisions you will make is where you and your family choose to worship. After arriving in Nashville TN several years ago I learned that I was going to have to position myself for making it home, immediately after acclimating myself with employment and housing I sought out for a church.

There were of course many fine churches to choose from I had to allow God to lead and guide me. What was most interesting with this particular church that I had finally visit for the several people that I had inquired about what church was good, this church, Mt Zion was not on the top of the list. In fact many people spoke against it, but what was most incredible was that all of their criticism lied in the facts of the size of the church and the type of car that the "Bishop" was driving which was a Bentley.

Now I have to be totally honest with you, I am not for anything that is not growing, in fact I will no longer invest in anything that is not growing and bearing fruit of return and especially a church while I am well known for being a strong philanthropist, I refuse to sow into anything that is not bigger than me.

Although the common plight with everyone was "I want to go to a church where my pastors knows me" I used to immediately respond with "don't you think it's more important for God to know you, I mean after all I doubt very seriously if any pastor your mother or father can VIP you to heaven".

Am I Your Enemy Because I Tell You The Truth?

In all seriousness I understood that they meant that they would just like more of a personal and hands on leader that is accessible. I must admit we all would like to have that to a degree.

Because of, not in spite of did I even the more wanted to visit this church. And "wow" was I floored almost instantly.

First off I just knew I was going to have to sit the pastor down and give him the whole stories as I have done with my other ½ siblings that my father had birth with other women besides my mother.

This pastor looked like my people on my father side what was most canny is that he even had certain attributes that we only possessed, my uncle Roger and him were literally like twins. I have often told people that come to me and swear that I look like their relative or close friend I usually reply with "my father was a rolling stone" or the other "it was a long boat ride for us all".

Beyond the fact of the obvious resemblance what was even greater "he got it", my soul had been searching for an anointed church that ministered with great teaching with nothing less than fundamental truth with a relevant and powerful word, and had balance, that will ultimately effect the community and the surrounding areas for which they claimed and solidified the territory for which they have been assigned to.

I was totally depleted upon my arrival in Nashville I had completed my divorce, closed up the business, and had just finished 2 speaking engagements. I did not go into the church tossing off my credentials or my long list of accomplishments. In fact I did not want anyone to know anything about me I just needed and wanted to know everything about God and where I was and where He wanted for me in this journey, I needed restoring and to be ministered to.

Post my divorce it was discovered that my husband had mishandled my funds along with my properties leaving me both destitute and homeless. Because of the contracts that I had with my business particularly with the "Girls residential unit", I could not afford to see them lost. I found a nearby house and literally squatted at this house for 3 months to complete that contract. I would got to my office and building daily in all its magnificent and functionality 5 star rooms for the girls by the grace of God. They were all filled and it is against policies among other things that I could not have stayed in a building that I both leased and ran for the purpose of assisting others, yet I needed assistance myself.

As fate would have it, while squatting at this house a local drug abuser actually turned the utilities on illegally for me and I was able to sustain myself during that time. When my son found out about it he came home from college and actually stayed with me for the remainder of that journey.

Nevertheless I arrived in Nashville with the attention of going to Atlanta within 2 month ....so I thought.

This pastor also in the beginning was very humble he had a combination of that of a nerd, unassuming, yet powerful all at the same time. There were moments that I can vividly see that he too was in his metamorphism experience both of life and ministry,

Am I Your Enemy Because I Tell You The Truth?

with the now loss of his wife and growth of the ministry all at the same time, he truly handled in the grace that only God could have given him. He even had strong supporters for whom I had admired throughout the years one being Bishop Paul Morton and Bishop GE Patterson these spiritual giants certainly solidify this now new pastor to me, what was interesting was that while yes he had a Bentley it was given to him by Bishop Paul Morton.

There were few Pastoral anniversary celebrations and when there was it was at the church with less than a third of the church in attendance and even then it was a short sermon and he thanking the church for allowing him to minster. His birthdays was he renting out a skating ring or a movie theater for the members to come out and just celebrate with him, even then there was not require gift or "offering" of him other than your presence. Though he was given the Bentley he actually would later sale and give the proceeds to the church. He was also accuse of stealing members from other churches.

That was the other lie, for anyone to even suggest that, they are first suggesting that those individuals have a mentally deficiency that they can without reason up and leave their church and go to another church that better fits them where they are now.

Besides only God is the Good Shepard, and the last I check all souls belong to him. So he can't steal sheep's but he can certainly grow grass.

Now I would never suggest that more means better; more money more problems, more people more problems. Just know that bigger churches suffer from the same things as smaller churches does just in larger scales. In fact you really want to count your members, call for a fasting and prayer hours and see how many show-up.

Call for cleaning the church or the community and see how many show up. What I can say though is that Bishop Walker has taken a many people towards the promise land. For you-would be Pastors that are driven to have mega churches I would say to you like Jesus said to the woman who wanted her sons to sit in the high place with God, "You Know NOT what you asked for!!!

The harsh reality is that some of us are spiritually abused in the very place where we should be receiving love and support, whether it's church leaders or other members. But you have to put this reality in proper perspective and allow truth to free you.

Remember that no church you attend is going to have the perfect pastor, the perfect co-pastor, the perfect choir director, the perfect Sunday school teachers, or the perfect members. Church, in some ways, is like a hospital, filled with sick people from the pulpit to the parking lot, who need God's help. Though we are believers, many of us still have issues we haven't overcome, and it affects how we treat those around us.

That's why it's wise to prayerfully consider where you receive your spiritual nourishment. Don't just choose a church because it has a fantastic choir or a good divorce-recovery program or because it has interesting activities for your children. Don't rely on how emotional you feel when you visit. Instead, seek God for where He wants you to plant yourself.

Am I Your Enemy Because I Tell You The Truth?

Church problems exist anywhere you go. But by following God's directions, He will lead you to the place where He can feed and nourish you best.

What is equally important of joining a church and giving of your substances (time, tithe, and talent), is the soil (foundation principles of that church.

Don't sow into "out of order churches", this will be comparable to continually putting in coins in a vendor machine hoping to receive a product and you getting nothing out of it, though you had consistently and loyally dedicate yourself to it you are getting nothing out of it, why on earth do you keep giving into anything that doesn't give back to you?

If you really check that vendor machine (place of worship) the "signs" were there all along, stop ignoring it.

It's out of order for a woman to take the place of the man of God and she leads with a bitter heart and tongue, it's out of order for a singer though skilled continually lead the choir yet harvest hate towards the people and their own mates, it's out of order for a leader in church use their title as an entitlement to behave viciously toward any people members or otherwise, it's out of order for man or women of God to teach love yet gossip and lie on one another and the body of Christ.

Why not just get somewhere as "the old folks will say, get somewhere and sat down", Just go and get healed, that you can minister effectively and relatedly because at the end of the day you can only redeem with that you can relate to in pure truth.

I'm not saying that your labor has gone unnoticed and you have in some way been faithful. The truth and reality is you have been called, chosen, given a measure of faith coupled with God's anointing. Your refusal to acknowledge and repent of your Achan-Joshua 7: (sin-accursed thing) will release a corporate curse with a contaminated anointing causing all victories to cease. The truth is it can be both a blessing and a curse being titled anything. There are heavy responsibilities, to whom much is given much is required.

It's amazing how people can envy the gift of anyone and never check the price tag of that gift.

Calvin and I have had haters that would hate on our many blessings and miracles. Some examples of their envy was our Community center. As nice as it was with all luxuries, and fine employees, and the numbers of people that attended our programs that included but not limited to job readiness, after-school programs, and live –in resident units for youth.

There was a burden keeping up codes and zoning, paying staff, producing the numbers of great programs, the many hours of labor and intense training involved. Our 4500 sq. ft. homes as nice as they are there it came with its burden with maintaining at times, you can see our gas bill and thought you saw our car notes.

Yes, we certainly are grateful for the many things that God has blessed us with, and they certainly did not add any sorrow to us.

Am I Your Enemy Because I Tell You The Truth?

What I am saying check out that price tag for the things you envy. You may not want or can afford it.

Among many other things the burdens and blessings always come together, I believe to keep us humble and balance, that we may relate to others.

Yes more folks do love the oil but they don't know the cost of your alabaster box.

To much is given much is required....

If my people who are called by my name shall humble themselves and pray, and seek my face, and turn from their wicked ways; then will I hear from heaven, and will forgive their sin, and will heal their land. II Chron. 7:14.

Our land is already in a state of emergency, we are in perilous times. I can assure you while God will bless us with things on this earth rim; from beautiful homes, church building, possessions, cars, businesses these temporal delights can never take the place of our eternal things such as our souls. In many of my prayer times the Lord has shifted my prayer will to turn to what matters to Him most, and that is His souls.

In many of my prayer times the Lord has shifted my prayer will to turn to what matters to Him most, and that is His souls.

It is a privileged to have Him the Lord of the universe and the God of all gods, the King of all kings, select you to share with you His heartbeat and passion, it is nothing less than both an honor and privilege.

When we are immersed with His Spirit and His agenda all things will fall into place and all things are good.

The hour is too late to be wrapped and tied up in foolishness, insignificant things and people are only mere distractions to take us off course, you got too much in you and territories to take over than to be stagnant on some temporal stuff.

One of my favorite Christian artists is Matthew West he has a song entitled "Do something", it goes with him charging God about all of the devastation going on in the world and why won't He do something? God said "I did **I created you**".

Could it be that you were chosen to make the difference that's needed from; immoral standards in the church or on your job, communities, warped mindsets of the world greatest asset our youth, the generational curses in your family, the illicit laws, the abuse towards Seniors, the fatherless, medical malpractices, the diluting of the word shared to the masses, destroy the lies in the now generation, if not you than who if not now than when?...We need you... Now.

You must know in advance that for every truth you come into the knowledge of you are held accountable for.

You will have to acknowledge Truth and its life-changing existence, yet the choice is still yours to make.

This will require a level of courage. It takes courage to walk away from the darkness of the lie and all of its residue. Sometimes living in the lie (dark) is just easier it doesn't require of you, it will not bother you provided you stay in it clinches. As a capture

Am I Your Enemy Because I Tell You The Truth?

animal in the jaw of a lion as long as it doesn't' move the lion will reduce its clutches.

The moment that captured prey set out to free itself the journey of it getting and staying loose is on.

Like cancer the lie is so intoxicating that it has contaminated all of your senses as a malignant growth it sets out to control your mind.

As a scene from a Zombie movie, once the plight of the lie enter your psychosis you are left with no hope for it will seduce you to your most lowest form it literally like a drug as harsh as crack cocaine will take you out of yourself into a unrecognizable human being. It sets out to control you leaving you with no resistance only becoming the monster that it is.

There are actually people who are on crack that though their body and essence have shivered away they believe (lie) they are still looking like they did before their first hit.

But when you open up to embrace and allow the truth to operate in your life it will power-on in your membrane and began to lose you from every strong hold causing yourself to see who you are now while processing to who you will become.

Tonya M. Thomas

CHAPTER 8
God's Specific Blessings Made With You in Mind

God has an abundance of blessings with your name on them.

"You really can have it before you have it," says Pastor Keith Vincent. He and his beautiful wife, Nicola, are the pastors of Greater Compassion Church.

It was a time in my life that truth was taking its course of setting me free, free from hidden agendas and dependence on certain things and individuals. One of the things I had to overcome was the act of impatience in that I had to give back and not hold on to anything that was not God-ordained.

This, my friend, may mean you have to give back some toys and trinkets that though they were desired, you may have to give them back because of the spirit attached to them.

I've had to give back cars, jewelry, engagement rings, and clothing.

"And whosoever will not receive you when you go out of that city shake off the very dust from your feet as a testimony against him" (Luke 9:5).

To get what you want, you must be prepared not to have it at all. You have to come to a place of thought that either I am going to get what I believe or nothing at all. This resilience is seen in every case where a person chose to obtain or die. Martin Luther King Jr., Andrew Young, and Harriet Tubman came to this resolve.

This is the formula for all things that are desired and to be obtained. "Give me liberty, or give me death." That is the question that only you can answer.

Everyone Needs a Big Bertha Experience

"Is anything too hard for the Lord? At the time-appointed I will return unto thee. Gen 18: 14-15

We all get weary and feel forsaken, like our patriarch Abraham and Sarah, the promise (desired fulfilled) for the two of them had its trial of patients. What was amazing God in His word did not mind sharing Sarah's or Abraham posture.

When given the promise Abraham, immediately showed a level of worship, humility, with expectation; Sarah like most of us in her weariness, faith has gotten low and just to hear about a promise that did not manifest in our time of expectation.

When reminded, we would go into a laugh of unbelief (privately that is, to save face among the "faithful) but God knew that and I believe though he honors our belief he is Father enough to sympathize with our weariness, but always Jehovah enough to perform that what he promised.

Am I Your Enemy Because I Tell You The Truth?

You might say, "Who is Big Bertha?" Well, let me introduce her. Big Bertha was a van that the Lord afforded me to possess through His kingdom (principles).

Let me explain. I was at this place in my life where I found my purpose for where ministry was birthed and developed, directions were certain, and events were concrete, and inevitably fruit was undeniable. That process was a result of my personal intimacy and desire for only God's Word. I could not nor can you ever be the same when having a sincere appetite for God's Word––the ultimate truth.

I was at a church for where the Word was forever preached, emotions were high, and discipline was taught as it relates to fasting and praying. Those formulas should never be underestimated when practiced.

At this point in our lives, my son and I did not own our own vehicle. I had come away from people and things that were not connected to my destiny, so of course that meant giving things back, no longer using ill content skill for possessions and impatience for a payback. But this meant to really trust in a God that I could not see from a man and a source that I could see.

My son and I had been picked up by someone who had carried us to church. This person had also picked up others as well. We had left a visiting church and, as usual, it was a great high time in the Spirit that the residue was still afloat. I was in this van and had an out-of-body experience.

Tonya M. Thomas

While looking out of the window, I saw this van. It was the newest van at the time, though the style was eye-catching and demanded a thorough glance. It was the thought that came with the glance, and that was this: My son, Calvin, and I founded a nonprofit organization entitled Children of the King. Children of the King is a community service organization that assists the homeless, provides recreational activities for the youth and continual care and services for seniors.

What I saw with the van was us utilizing the van for the organization. Now you must know that at this time I was actually laid off, and here I was looking at a new van with no income. Later that night, Calvin and I were in prayer, and God confirmed this vision through Calvin and gave both of us such an excitement and a thrill that we could not even sleep that night.

Immediately with that spiritual confirmation, I got on the way with receiving this manifestation. I called a good friend and sister in the Lord to take me to this dealership. As I reflect, I can see this was purpose on who I took with me. This is a lesson you must keep: When you are believing God for something, you can't tell everyone, and you shouldn't because they can either be a blessing or a hindrance for your miracle.

Meanwhile, my friend came and picked me up, and off we went. I had nothing less than high expectancy, and I was literally giddy because I thought that meant I was just going to pick it up that day because that's how my faith/belief worked. But let's just say God had His plan in action.

Am I Your Enemy Because I Tell You The Truth?

So I met this nicely groomed and articulate salesperson. He was very sharp and welcoming as he approached me.

"How can I assist you today?"

I immediately shared with him the description of the van I was interested in, and he shared how they just got so many in recently and all their gadgets. As he was concluding his sales approach, and after the tour and the test drive, we finally sat at his desk to hash out all the particulars.

"Well, I am excited for all of this excitement you have brought in with you. You got even the more excited as we went to see the selection, and you said that the color was what you had in mind. You also said that you are of a surety that particular van is what you have come to get. You were adamant about not viewing a used van but a brand-new van. I must say I've never had anyone with this much enthusiasm for a van and even the more for what your plans are for its use. So let me assist you with driving on out today as you have said you would like to do today."

Now this is where he brought out all of the paperwork and documents necessary, for I had already assured him that I planned on driving out that day. He had even gotten out temporary plates, insurance for me to cover, and finally even a couple of extra perks that included but were not limited to fragrance for the car, a scraper, and dealership paraphernalia.

Because of my persistent resolve and my posture, I looked and acted as if I had a billion dollars to just give away. The salesperson could have only assumed that he was not wasting his time, and he could actually spend his commission in his head already because I was a sure sale——until . . .

"So how would you like to pay for this?"

With confidence and boldness, I replied, "I don't have any money, but God said it was mine."

The salesperson replied, "Ma'am, I believe in God, too, but you got to have some money."

I said, "Yes, that might be true, but the Lord said that van is mine, and I have come to retrieve it."

The look in his eyes at that very moment was that of both anger and frustration, coupled with the thought of searching for a phone number to call the crazy home and tell them, "One of your patients is missing and is sitting in front of me, so please come and get her, or let me call the police, for this thief has come and has stolen my time and skills!"

Even with his infuriation, he professionally cut short the presentation and said, "I will keep your information, and we will see what we can do. We will call you."

I emphatically and joyously replied, "OK, I will be waiting."

Now here is where the journey begins. I must tell you I was not only laid off from work, but I did not have the best credit report. My son was in private school, and I had a mortgage. Now even as I'm typing this, those were my miracles that preceded this.

Although on the surface I was a single parent (my son's father was deceased, and I had no financial support in place), I had a mortgage. I owned a home in a community where everyone had

Am I Your Enemy Because I Tell You The Truth?

two incomes and two parents, but my family wasn't financially supportive. In fact, we were the ones to whom the family came for support. Yet I was believing for a brand-new van.

God had already shown His power with those witnesses alone. My son was in private school his whole life, and I did not miss a payment. We had a four-bedroom home in a high-end and affluent community, and even now that house was paid off. Even with our financial circumstances, we were feeding people who were homeless but catching the bus to take them lunches and clothes, and I was unemployed.

This is where you understand your true source. You will operate in life on a different vibration.

So I moved forward with the vision and plan unfiltered with hope that God was going to bring it through. Now in this process, you come quickly with the thought that you don't know how He's going to bring it to pass. You just believe that He is true to His word. You may not know what method He is going to use to do it, but you will later—not necessarily at that time—appreciate His process.

So days went by, and I had my son continually touching and agreeing with me. We were the real "wonder twin powers," and we had activated so many other things; but this was a set-up to build our powers for greater spiritual strength and possession.

Please understand though when I say "possession." Don't limit this to the tangible alone (cars, houses, jewelry, and clothing). Calvin and I had seen through our touching and agreeing through love (God) kings' hearts changed, souls saved, deliverance of people on drugs and sex, minds changed, laws softened for our common good, generation of nonsense in our families come to a complete halt never to return, and people by the masses joined our causes.

Because we are in part of our three beings, our human side became weary. Ultimately, I had Calvin at a place where he would race home expecting to see the van in the driveway. In fact, on many occasions while in prayer, Calvin and I walked around our driveway and declared it, so much so that we gave it life through our belief way before we were able to see, touch, and handle it.

We came to our weary days. Calvin running home with high expectations came to a minimum. In fact, one day, he came home, and I said in an excited voice, "Calvin, about the van . . ." and he immediately interrupted me with, "Yeah, yeah, Mom. I know. Not yet, but its coming. Right, Mom?" Because we were so connected (twins in the Spirit), I too had become weary. But I did not want him to know, and I always wanted him to trust in God but not the process.

And the process is really all that counts. The process is what gives your Big Bertha (blessing) its authenticity.

You may be looking for and expecting Him to show up in a traditional type of way. Well, let me tell you, our God will break, not bend, some rules for you. Because He's God, He can change policies. He can fast-track an ordinary process. He can use complete strangers you don't know nor do they know you, but they have to turn around and bless you. Maybe they won't even stay around, but they were only there for the purpose of coming up to you and writing you a check for a million dollars. And your only responsibility is to just receive it with gratitude.

God says His ways are not our ways nor are His thought like our thoughts. Aren't you glad about that? Because there are some family members, friends, and all from whom you would really rather not borrow, loan, or be the recipient of anything they have, though you are in great need of it. Not all people, but there are some who, even though you may pay them back, you will owe them for the rest of your life. But our God frees us from any bondage or challenge of the blessing because, after all, His blessings "maketh rich and he addeth no sorrow with it."

Trust me. God's blessings last longer, and they carry a level of peace. Even when they're tangible, they're so enjoyable because of the intent of the Giver. God had only you in mind to bring a blessing to you that was assured of nothing lacking or broken on levels upon levels of joy. In fact, I'm not sure that without it you can really appreciate the gift.

In most cases, many people who have been given anything with substance and value but did not pay a price for it or had to endure some patience through it cannot really appreciate it because it did not cost them anything. For you Christians who are bent on taking the "humble approach" will say, "Jesus paid it all." But you forget that while salvation is free, it cost God His everything.

Tonya M. Thomas

Being a believer takes a strong courageous person. It's not for the weak and feeble. This will ultimately separate the boys and the men, the girls and the women. This is ultimately a proving ground.

Well, time had lapsed. I did not hear from the car representative. Mind you, I did not have a personal car, so while all my desire was to be a blessing to others by getting this van, I personally did not have access to a vehicle. I only had one child, and really Calvin and I did not need a van. I could have possibly gotten a small vehicle, and that would have sufficed; but Calvin and I were always concerned about someone else other than ourselves.

Even with our four-bedroom home, we did not need a four-bedroom home; but in the thought of being a blessing to others, as we did constantly, we had a four-bedroom home. There was always someone who needed a place to stay, and we afforded them their need in love and shared our home. I have had uncles, aunties, brother and sisters, my father, friends, and people needing immediate shelter from abused relationships, hard financial times, or just transition who came and stayed in our home.

I say all of this because your tangible gift/blessing would never separate you from your character. If you were selfish in your one-bedroom, you will be selfish in your four-bedroom. If you were selfish with $100, making you a millionaire will only make you a selfish millionaire. If you were trifling and unfaithful with a relationship with a potential mate and friends with two people, you will be the same with the masses and with a serious relationship.

Am I Your Enemy Because I Tell You The Truth?

If you did not do well on your job and did less than average, giving you your own business will only make it a less-than-average business. If you are not kind to your own family and children, you can't be genuinely kind to strangers. If you are not faithful to yourself, you can't be faithful to another. If you don't pay tithes on $10, you will not pay tithes on a million dollars. In other words, if you are not faithful over a few things, how can God make you ruler over much?

In our time of growing weary, we then began to take the focus of that part of our dilemma and focus on the things we could handle. We continued with what we knew we could do. We still kept the course of our ministry because God saw our relentlessness and our faith to keep on, even by catching buses to drop off lunches and clothing to the homeless in the downtown area of our city.

We than began to request help from others and, boy, did they come! We had so much help from assisting and transporting our needs as well that we did not miss a beat. Now I am not saying that it did away with the frequent feelings of hurt and disappointment. To really know Calvin and me, while we were great givers, we were also strongly independent. We did not like depending on anyone. Calvin and I would really go without before asking others. Some concluded that was a sign of pride, but I have to disagree.

I grew up as the oldest, and many responsibilities fell on me early in life, which included but were not limited to babysitting, cooking, cleaning, grocery shopping, and helping my siblings with their homework. Calvin grew up as an only child in a single-parent house, and he, too, had his share of responsibilities early in his life that included but were not limited to sometimes waking himself up on time for school, making it to his sports practices on time, going to piano lessons on time, heating up his food, and sometimes doing his own homework without any assistance.

When you have had no assistance, you become self-reliant, not necessarily proud. You literally know no other way. On top of that, you add to the fact that others depend on you because you have shown yourself to be dependent. But all the while, many can depend on you, you yourself have not had many on whom you can depend on. This all makes you the more self-sufficient, and Calvin and I never allowed any of those challenges to make us bitter. In fact, it only made us better.

While the wait pressed on, Calvin and I were being made perfect in our weakness, and patience was doing what it does best: beating and shaping us into perfection (maturity). Let's just say a newer foundation was being tested and laid. Do you know that a faith that cannot be tested cannot be trusted? Calvin and I were tested and were found true.

I recall my being called back for work for one month. During this time, I was two weeks in to catching the bus to get to work, only to be on my feet for the course of the day because at that time I was a mail-carrier.

I was on a fast, and as my practice during my fast, not only would I not eat, but I believed in not reading anything except Scripture. This afforded me a level of strength mentally and physically. I had

Am I Your Enemy Because I Tell You The Truth?

gotten up at 4:00 a.m. and had begun my routine of both studying and praying God's Word and declaring my day. Later, I walked my son to my neighbor's house and proceeded on to the bus stop. When I think back, it is so amazing because during this time, it was about 6:00, and it was still dark, but I never had any fear as I was walking by myself (physically) to a bus in the city of Detroit. I just have to say as a side note: Reading the Word of God will truly give you not only peace and a sound mind, but a level of courage.

I concluded my day of work and, to my surprise, I got the greatest favor. I finished my task two hours before time and was blessed to be offered to leave early yet get paid for a full day.

Wow! As a letter-carrier for the post office, that was comparable to someone hitting the lottery. I was like, *Wow, this is just God's favor!*

I clocked out and ran to the bus station so I could get home. I got to the bus stop, high with joy and peace, and then the unforeseen occurred. I was waiting at the bus stop, and not only did the bus not come as scheduled, but it was 45 minutes late. This had never occurred and was by far not the norm.

I was at the bus stop for going on two hours, and not only had the weather grown hotter than normal, but I was faced with my sweat and the heat, and now I was tired and weary. While many cars were riding by me with their favorite songs, I was trying to sing a spiritual song in my mind before I totally got wiped out by the defeat of my weariness because at this point I was watching people ride by me who I know were not serving God, yet they were not only driving, but they were driving good.

Here I was trusting in a God I could not see, and I could really make some calls and call on a man that I could see. This just was not fair, and it was a smack in my face and my faith because I was fighting over something that was not only an essential part of everyone's life, but I was also holding off to be a blessing for others. And these people riding by me, in more cases than not, had only themselves on their minds.

Wow! What kind of God was I really serving? Did He care? Was He a sadist? Why on earth did He bless me to get off early only for me to wait two hours at a bus stop? What was really going on?

I had come to the conclusion to just take a cab and use the money that was my lunch/emergency money and pay for it. You have to know that this time for cell phones was not as popular, so I had to wait until I saw a cab to flag it down. Finally, one arrived. I was so weary that I could not wait to get home and have my private gut-busting cry.

I got into this cab, and the cab driver was so jubilant that it was aggravating. I thought to myself, *If he says another positive thing, I am going to scream!* Now I have to tell you he was of a Jamaican sect, and his native tongue only added to his jubilancy that demanded extra attention. He finally realized that he was not going to get a corresponding conversation from me, so he got quiet.

Finally, during the drive, he began to hum a gospel song called "I Got a Message from the Lord, Hallelujah." As he hummed, my

Am I Your Enemy Because I Tell You The Truth?

spirit immediately stood at attention and joined him. Now mind you, I said my spirit. My flesh was still at a place that just wanted to get home and run to my quiet place and release my tears.

I got home and immediately stripped myself of my sweaty clothes and got to one of my therapies: showering. As I was showering, the miracle took place. I was first showering, but as the water was coming down, my tears were coming down even faster.

As I was showering, an angel came to me, and immediately there was first a peace. And, suddenly, he spoke and told me first that the Lord loves me and to fear not because He was going to bless me. I was so immediately arrested in this uncontrollable joy that I leaped out of my shower and began to run around my home praising God. I just thank God my blinds were closed!

I was so excited that I later called my mother, who to be a Christian, had known that I was believing God for my van. When I called her with such excitement, she thought I had received it.

"Mom, oh my God, oh my God! My van!"

"You got it?"

"No, not yet, but God told me He is going to do it."

Her reply was comparable to the ghost in the Pacman video game because she said "Oh" in a really unbelieving and cynical way.

"Oh, that's nice baby. I'm happy for you."

Not only did I get a valuable lesson, but I also knew then that she was not designed to be part of my faith crew. You cannot always share your truth with everyone, including family and close friends.

Tonya M. Thomas

There are some people who want to believe God with you, but they do not share the level of faith you have. Understand that is OK.

In the scheme of things, God will trust your life to increase their faith. You may only get one person to whom you can touch and agree with in believing for your victory and even the more have only your best interest in mind and sincerely want to see you blessed, even if it's not his or her turn. As a believer, trust and believe. We do not serve a limitless God. He will never run out of blessings for His people.

Later, when my son came home, I shared my experience with him, and he was just as excited as I was. Thank God for Jesus, though, that I had my son humanly to share this experience with. You may not have anyone physically with whom you can entrust your experience, but you will always have someone spiritually you can trust, for Jesus is the great Intercessor and Friend who sticks closer than a brother.

Weariness had a stronghold, but faith came in and won the battle. I can't tell you just when it happened, but what became my sign of deliverance and victory is **when it did not matter anymore.** I had come to a place where I was no longer consumed, feeling the need to justify it any longer.

After all, we were talking about a genuine need and an essential need for Calvin and me. But when we really let it go, it no longer had its hold on us. I am a strong believer of having things but not things having me.

Am I Your Enemy Because I Tell You The Truth?

I was finally able to rest, not just sleep with anxiety, but rest, and this was my first sign of the shift. Calvin's smile was back, but this time he had a new swag that suggested he was on another Plato. My smile returned as well as if to say we were good for real. Now you must understand that by this time, we had shared our news with some people we thought in sincerity would be glad for us. We also had to get that lesson.

Just know that everyone, even while you are believing for something/someone, will not always share your happiness, even though you have genuinely shared theirs. These haters are not limited to people on the outside, but they may include those who share your last name, look like you, attend your church, and share the same faith. They might have been your friends for years; grown up with you; were your prayer partners; and, yes, they may even be your own leader, spiritual and otherwise.

Not everyone is going to embrace your Big Bertha experience, and that's OK. But God will send you first His comforter and His angels, and He can also send you His choice of person/people during the process.

I was out a particular day, and I was out with God's choice person in my life. At this time, this sister was a walking faith cheerleader. This incredible anointed woman of God was named Gwendella Burkes, aka Sister Gwen. She and I would come together in sheer bliss when we prayed and believe in God to do things in each other's lives. We would both unselfishly pray and intercede for each other with high expectations for each other to succeed in our individual journeys.

Tonya M. Thomas

There was never any jealousy, ill will, or envy of any sort. We genuinely and authentically wanted nothing less than the best for each other. Gwen was very secure within herself, as I was very secure within myself, and we both can genuinely respect and love others as well.

There were so many times when we would get together and there would just be this excitement. I say this because it is imperative not just while you desire to possess something but even for everyday life that you keep positive people in your circle. Your words and words that can be stimulated by those around you can make the difference on your outcome––good, bad, indifferent, or simply delayed.

Gwen and I would meet each day with doable and obtainable goals in mind, all with a subtle fuel of joy that neither one of us could explain. We both shared looks from others as if something was wrong with us with this joy, although they all knew everything was right about us.

In fact, it was so right it was often contagious, but it always demanded a level of attention.

This particular time, both Gwen and I were out, and while we were together, we came across someone of like-spirit. This gentleman not only took our attention, but he introduced himself and his business.

He looked and talked like a child of the King. He not only confirmed it by his conversation, but his spirit preceded his conversation. When he gave us his business card, it turns out he

Am I Your Enemy Because I Tell You The Truth?

worked for the same dealership where I had gone to claim my van. I shared with him that I had gone there some time ago and how I believed that God told me to go there and possess. And here's where it got real. He said to me, "Do you still believe"?

I paused and replied emphatically, "Yes!"

He said, "It is well."

He set up an appointment with me. I met with him and explained all of my current circumstances, although I did not do that the first time. He simply replied, "It's not a problem" and "Don't worry about anything. You did say you believed, right?"

I said yes, and he said, "All is well. I will get back with you soon."

Our meeting lasted every bit of 12 minutes, with five of those minutes consisting of him sharing a testimony of God's grace in his life. He concluded by saying, "Just let me serve you."

Seven days later, I was at home in a complete nap (divine rest), and I got a phone call. It was my salesperson (divine angel), and he said with excitement, "Come and get your van!" I said, "Thank you," and I went back to finish my nap. Upon finishing my nap, I took a moment to write some Scriptures down to take to the first salesperson because I knew I was assigned to. After arriving, I embraced my now current salesperson (angel/ brother in the Lord). It turns out that he was the well-respected and number one man in the place. He dressed well and had such a posture that many people who came into his presence and office humbled themselves as if he were the king himself. Not only was he "the man" of the place, he was "a man of God." To this day, I don't know what he did.

All I know is I did not put down any money. I was laid off of work with no promising day of return. My debt ratio said real loud, "Don't even try it!" yet I was signing papers to receive the brand new van. I rejoiced, and he rejoiced with me because I had sowed with so many tears, and I doubtless came back with my vehicle rejoicing.

After concluding our business and leaving his office, I found the first salesperson I had met. I went to his desk and showed him my keys and proclaimed to him, "See, I told you that our Father, the Lord Jesus Christ, told me he was going to give me this van."

He looked at me with shock and fear and said, "Oh, yes, I'm happy for you. I, I knew you would get it."

This was all said with great shudder and amazement. I then proceeded to give him the list of Scriptures and told him to please read and enjoy. He received them, and I shook his hand, and that was it––or so I thought.

My van, to which my son Calvin and I had given the name Big Bertha, got on the road of ministry. We were taking many souls to church, and we were caravanning with other people who joined us to hand out clothes and food to the homeless on the streets. We were increasing in so many areas in our lives, as well as others.

Three months later, on one of our feeding crusades, as I was handing out food and clothes and praying and hugging and just demonstrating love as God would have me to do, I looked up

Am I Your Enemy Because I Tell You The Truth?

at a circle of men that was on the corner. I looked around as I was concluding prayer and saw the first salesperson from the van dealership.

I almost did not recognize him because when I first met him, he had a shiny suit and was well-groomed. Now he had on clothing that not only was not well cared for, but he was homeless and all that comes with being homeless.

As Calvin and I were passing out the food and clothing out of Big Bertha, we gave the man extra. I hugged him longer than any of the other people, and he held me with tears.

I assured him that he would be OK because our Father Lord Jesus Christ had him, and it would get better. Three months later, that same brother joined our ministry and was one of our best laborers.

More often than not, your blessings are not always just about you. But God will always get His glory, and you and I can be the privileged, fortunate, and trusted conduits who can be used for His tasks.

Just remember, it's not always about you, but it always is about His glory. Selah.

God knows each of us so intimately that He knows exactly how and when to bless us. So when He fashions His choice blessings for us, they're not random or without significance. When God blesses us, He gives us specific blessing that are just for us.

Tonya M. Thomas

**The greatest Gift of my life...
my son Calvin**

When a woman is pregnant, she experiences the evolution of a life, a life that will consist of a spirit, a soul, and a body. When I was pregnant with my son, Calvin, I could have never imagined what was to come. How do you describe in words the ultimate blessing of your life? Oftentimes you find that the English vocabulary is so limited and cannot adequately express how you feel.

Am I Your Enemy Because I Tell You The Truth?

It was 1987. I was pregnant with Calvin, and his father was out of town. I had spent time with my grandfather, but I wasn't feeling well, so he took me to the doctor. After a false alarm, I felt better and thought I would be fine. But later, I felt sharp pains, and my grandmother told me that I needed to go to the hospital immediately. While en route, Grandma started singing the "It's Time" song, which was one song I wasn't ready to hear.

But she was right. On May 15, 1987, after three long hours of labor, my son Calvin was born. Someone called his father, and he made his way back to town. Though the pain was indescribable, when that little life came forth, I was in complete awe.

Up to that point, I had experienced many wonderful things, but nothing could compare to the moment Calvin was born. And like most mothers think of their children, I thought my son was the most beautiful baby in the world.

I am just eternally grateful that God would afford his father and me to be the conduits of such a masterpiece. For Calvin's physical attributes everyone had their claims Calvin's father could claim his head, lips, and ears, everyone knew hands down that Calvin had my nose, his grandmothers complexion, he had his great grandmother hair, his great grandfather hands, my father actually said "I knew Calvin was my grandson when I changed his diaper"….. Well let's just say I often wonder what made my mother stayed as long as she did. Calvin truly had the eyes of our Lord Jesus Christ. When he would look at you it was as if he looked right through you.

Tonya M. Thomas

Though Calvin had many of mines and his father family's' physical features, it was his loving smile and his eyes that captured the hearts of most people. When he looked at you, it was as if he were looking through you. I immediately knew he had our heavenly Father's eyes.

We were blessed to have Calvin at one Michigan finest hospital, William Beaumont. This very upscale hospital though known for its excellent doctors had even a greater reputation of its patience care.

All parents were given a fine dinner and gifts to celebrate their new- born. This five course meal included filet mignon, my grandfather joined us in the festivities. This was his first time having filet' mignon.

You have never heard filet' mignon pronounced until you have heard my granddaddy pronounce it. He goes "Chicken (my pet name he gave me) this is the best filaugha migaer I've ever had"…. After many attempts to pronounce it correctly everyone just accepted the new name of filet mignon……for now on, no one can call it by that name the new name of it for us all is" filaugha migaer" (smile).

Because of an allergic reaction, I had to remain in the hospital for an additional three weeks. During that time there was such a traffic of people, all of my visitors, as well as the nursing staff, spoiled Calvin. Even strangers would come by just to see him!

I thought that after a few days the newness would wear off and I would settle into the humdrum routine of motherhood, but that

Am I Your Enemy Because I Tell You The Truth?

never happened. Each day brought new experiences and a feeling of joy and excitement. Although others were vying to hold Calvin and keep him entertained, when I had him all to myself, I fell in love with him all over again.

During those three long weeks in the hospital, often I was in pain because of various tests. But when they would bring in Calvin, none of that mattered. All my pains would subside, and I felt nothing but peace. He was my healing. I was amazed that God loved me so much that he gave me the most incredible and unconceivable blessing, the greatest gift––life.

Calvin came out and always had an old soul. He never impressed easily, hardly anything moved him, accept those things that he held to heart. The things that he held to heart deeply was first family, his friends, the human race and his array of pets.

Because I personally never was given a birthday party from my parents my entire life, giving my son a birthday party was very important to me. I have through-out the years were very creative with the celebration of his birth from Chuck E cheese, Major magic, to hotel parties with limousine rides with access to video games, laser tags, Concerts with Special Guest appearances and back-stage passes.

But I remember a time though where I knew I was going to get "the look of great approval", because for me it was always in the wow factor of him because, again he did not impress easily. I guess with looking back I had always did things non-traditionally with him, I actually went from celebrating him every 2 months then when he became a 1 yr. old I went traditionally every year so maybe he partied out early.

There was one time where I had to redefine my entire approach of his parties. This particular birthday I had been eyeing this huge telescope because of his then strong interest in Science, for his birthday gift.

That birthday theme was centered on space and stars, and literally stars. I had a planned a birthday party with a sleep-over at our local park, I had gotten a lot of tents and sleeping bags and all of the gadgets for a space theme, I had even got a friend who owned a local party store who not only assisted me with themes but had some left over fireworks from a huge sale, so it really was a party with a bang.

With all of the guest that included but not limited to family, his neighborhood associates, church members, and class mates. We had always had huge and over the top events for him, while I did not get the wow factor I was hoping for I always got the appreciation for everything for he was always grateful for everything, regardless of its size and capacities. What occurred that I had learned was that he loved the theme and of its gadgets but he did not care for the crowd.

Calvin learned early on, to not count people in your life by the quantity of numbers but the quality in numbers. He advised me that not everyone in attendance was there for him/ or his celebration nearly as much as they were there for the excitement. By no means was Calvin ever arrogant or narcissistic in anyway, but he knew

Am I Your Enemy Because I Tell You The Truth?

early on not everyone is deserving of your time or you celebration. I learned that much, later I only wish I could have been so smart. Calvin had a very strong entrepreneur spirit, I nor his father can take all of the credit, but his great grandfather on his father side, Mr. Easley literally owned several grocery stores, rental property, and was a Minister in Gadsden, Alabama.

Calvin had many business growing up beginning at the age of seven, from his lawn services, car washes, and seniors' assistance. What stood out most was his special attention to details, he was a perfectionist and always believed that he was writing his signature on everything he did. He always was a person of timing, late for him was 20 min early. I have to say he did not get that from me nor his father.

Calvin's heart was just beyond words he would give without any reservations and always genuinely concern about the next person often more than himself. Although he was very studious, beyond his years of maturity and intellect, he took integrity to new and unfounded heights, he was very comedic.

My already growing up with my siblings of which came with our in-home personal entertainment. I have to say the greatest gifts my parents could have ever giving me were my siblings I truly love them more than words can express. They were the ultimate die-hard fans of comedic expressions. I was already prepared for any style he chose of and even create some new ones.

Calvin and I would prank one another and I will give him an (in-house sister) version. So he would actually get a mom first and foremost of me, sister, friend, confidant, prayer partner, and comedic challenger.

I recall once when he was dating as I so often did I would give his dates nick-names in my (sister version). There was this one young lady, that he brought over that let's just say you would not have to ask her rather or not she had milk, for she literally had breast for days . When introduced of her I did not know rather or not to shake her hand or her breast for they both were reaching out to me.

I would then try to embarrass him, just doing things that a playful younger sister would-do, the kind of things I endured with my siblings. Calvin always shared with a good sense of humor. The joy we would bring to one another all the time spewed to anyone who either met us or came around. In many of his comedic stands and ways what would always be so delightful was his timing and energy, it will always leave you in stitches.

What I love most of my son is his fearlessness of embracing his entire self. He was a man that was in full charge and awareness of himself and grown in all his awareness. Although he was my son he had the ability of sharing a father-like attributes because he was so protective, concretely corrective, sharp in his intuitiveness, daring and calculated in his ingenuity.

Like, Calvin's father Mr. Tony Easley Jr. handsome is in their genes, but with many people did not know about his father was that although he was highly popular for his looks his mind was far more attractive and the acclaim was their divergent thinking.

Am I Your Enemy Because I Tell You The Truth?

These incredible minds were before their times and times were yet trying to catch up with them.

Calvin has always affectionately called me twin and it wasn't just that we physically favored nearly as much as alike we are in so many ways both spiritually and mentally our heartbeats and passions of interest were alike where like natural twins we would actually finish each other thoughts without saying a word.

On many occasion he was my higher me, always willing to challenge me to stay in the higher me while always lovingly build me up when I was low. Many people who has been blessed to be in his presence can attest to the fact that he can know the least and always say the most.

My natural mother will often tell me that "everyone does not think like you!" What was most interesting she would say this in the most condescending way, giving off the impression that it was something wrong with me?

When the reality was I just did not think like her or the majority of the people she knew. With Calvin's father now passing when Calvin was seven yrs old I knew I would have to work harder.

I personally would encourage my son to think and even the more expose him to many other things to even consider in forming his thoughts while shaping his beliefs. I always believed that we can never go any further than our thoughts "so a man thinketh so is he".

Tonya M. Thomas

Am I Your Enemy Because I Tell You The Truth?

Tonya M. Thomas

There were many times that my son thought that I was overbearing with the heights I would believe he can go because I always believed that there were no limits. I like most mothers of great nurture would take great pride of having myself heavily involved in his life yet also gave him some space to explore and master his journey of manhood.

All the while most of the times I would considered all the pitfalls that were dangerously out in this world and would go into a mad mother bear syndrome, if I thought he was close to a pitfall or an individual or people were trying to set him up for one. I believe that God Himself has equipped mother's with a strong sense to smell the danger of someone or something coming against their children which why I could instantly tell Calvin as well what friends, were not good, or what girlfriends were not worth two dead flies.

There were only a few occasions he would have the challenge of not seeing through these people. But for the few times his vision got blurred on the account of trusting people for whom should have had his best interest.

My natural sister husband for whom had a past of being a local small drug dealer in our hometown neighborhood, was one of the individuals for whom he trusted that could have cost him his liberty.

At a time where like all young men who are coming into themselves, bad choices are made and they become very rebellious towards their parents, this journey that every young man travels while earning their rights of passage of manhood all while being very impressionable, would come at a high cost but provided the seed that were sown in their lives from conception on up can and will make all the world of differences on how it can play out.

I thank God through His word who promises that "when you train up a child the way he should go; and when he is old, he will not depart from it "Proverbs 22:6. It did not say that they would not stray but they will not depart. Believe me there is a difference between departing and straying, remember straying will always return, trust the God of His word. What occurred, unbeknownst me, I thought the lifestyle that my natural sister and her husband had lived was no longer, I thought that he had left that lifestyle and was no longer in any fashioned engaged in it. Little did I know not only he was very much involved but his old friend of his not only came to the South but thought they would bring up their old ways again and recruit my son with it.

My natural sister and I relationship has always been strained as she grew older ,I had to learned very quickly that she was who she was and it will be to my best interest to truly love her from a distance. I somehow believed that while her jealousies and dislike towards me would not pour over into my son.

Though she has through-out the years showed very little respect and concern towards me, I have always showed it towards her and especially towards her children.

I unlike her and many others believe to keep children out of your web of deceit and lies and unresolved issues. I have always believe in protecting their innocence, also there are two different relationships and should be handled as such.

This is the same man that she married who was the best friend of the boyfriend that she had longed dated and she herself was a good friend of the girl to whom he dated a longtime, their affair occurred all while their mates were unaware, but to add injury to insult she would get pregnant and was unsure as to who the father was yet my beautiful niece Bria was born and that is the gift, however she lied to the natural father (former boyfriend) who had other children, to whom my niece looks just like him and have other siblings, yet my sister prefer to stick to her lies.

You see people who go unchecked to their vicious insulting way literally carry the greater lie and are themselves being deceived all while they are attempting to deceive others. The lie itself has captivated them so, that they believe they are in control and somehow gotten over. When the truth of the matter they have and will always only fool themselves. You see my sister had always practiced this type of ill-will, the sad part about it is that she was always exposed. Most times from her own acquaintances.

There were times like the movie "Coming America" the eldest sister obviously with charm, intellect, and lastly looks had presence. The younger sister convinced herself that she was second fiddle and would secretly attempt to be with the would-be pursuer of her older sister.

Am I Your Enemy Because I Tell You The Truth?

For where envying and strife is, there is confusion and every evil work. James 3:16

These continually viscous acts that my natural sister has shown towards myself, brothers, and other individuals, will always have her season of reaping. What my sister knows like all of my natural family knows, if I was to ever respond to her and her husband the way that at a time that I have been known to do these stories would be a lot different and I can promise you I would have to add murder on my resume. You must know the dog can bark at the moon all night, but if the moon was to ever bark back at the dog it will take national acclaim.

The fact is when you embrace truth you have no choice but to grow up that doesn't totally dismiss "the (enemy-in-a me) me I was and am yet dying to, it does suggest that I'm daily dying and growing at the same time. The fact also is that I do have an anger that can be explosive and costly to all involve, for protective purposes only.

This would serve as the case of my natural sister, I can share several stories of all her attempts.

In much of her narcissistic ways she convinced herself that she got a way and found some pleasure in the acts of her deceit. It will behoove her that many of her acts all came back to me, from her own friends to the guys themselves. I must tell you, you will be surprise of your witness; when people who"knew me when", learned of my response and my not doing (take her out) my sister.

It only furthered served as a witness towards God. They knew and couldn't deny that God was real. As many who "knew me when" can attest that was the result supernaturally I have taken people out, by fights for less. Not to retaliate, was not my strength and I will never tell you that I was not tempted..........but God.

I often like most confident people who trust the process find greater joy in watching these would-be haters simply do themselves. Like a dog chasing his tail, with all the attempts of my sister, trying to dress, act, befriend my associates, emulate me in all measures; she was not me and cannot be me. While it is true, imitation is the sincerest form of flattery. She was and will always be a cheap copy of a great original.

I have to trust God process and His way, there is a God who promises that vengeance belongs to him He would repay.

My mother has birth four children neither me nor my brothers have suffered from medical challenges of any sort, yet my natural sister stays in the hospital, the child that her husband and her birth stays in the hospital as well, and has had so many neardeath experiences his health challenges are both abnormal and viciously challenging, yet my brothers and I and our children have never suffered from unhealthy diagnosis.

The same guy she cheated with and married also continually cheats with other women.

My purpose of sharing that is to not be their judge but to simply remind me, why I would not have thought that they would be or serve of any moral value to my son. You never involve your family and especially children into any form of nonsense.

These disloyal, betrayal and antagonist human beings left me with a very bitter taste towards them. To be perfectly honest, while though being a Christian and practicing forgiveness I do not nor have any plans on ever having any form of relationship with neither of these individuals nor can careless to form any bonds in any form.

When I learned of what he did with my son and to know that my sister had some involvement only furthers the position that I stand on and that is not having anything to do with either. You see in truth even when it hurts because the devastation of such betrayals from people we are not required to continually place ourselves in harm's way with their evil intents.

I have several nieces including her daughter and nephews even with my siblings I have had lifestyles in my very early teenage years that I will never include even my sibling let along their children in any illegal activities of any sort, that was the lowest that anyone can go. When it came down to my son, that was totally it.

You have to take a firm stand in humility and let those individuals know that you will not tolerate nor continually receive from them their blatant negative ways towards you or your children. I suggest that you seek God and always pray first that He can lead you for an opportune time. Many people do not love confrontation, this is why you must first pray and seek God.

In most instances people like this is in denial, they may not readily accept their responsibility immediately they may very well shun it and retaliate to you and make it your fault. You must know however in the midnight hour when they are left to themselves they are often dealt with, no peace, no joy, no rest. You see the stuff that people like my sister and her husband got away with always has a way of coming back demanding its consequences.

That's OK, believe me I am a strong believer when you do your part, hurt and all, frustrated and all, even crying and all, angry and all.

God will reward you and you will gain both spiritually, financially, favorably in so many accounts.

I am a true witness I have seen God work oftentimes faster than I can blink. Rather he immediately reveals or not He is dealing with their hearts and because of your obedience He will award you first and foremost with his priceless peace. This does not dismiss the people to whom caused you pain or hurt. But God will grant you your hearts desires. He will restore that which was lost, replace and restore you with other healthy relationships.

This is why God says "who is my mother who is my brethren but them that do the will of my Father, that's my mother and brethren". I would learn very quickly as you should as well, that God knows everything. He will bless you with the desires of your heart. Though I would always have love for my sister and always love having a sister, I chose to hold on to the few good times that I have shared with her.

Am I Your Enemy Because I Tell You The Truth?

Everyone skin to me is not necessarily kin to me!

God has placed women in my life that has been the sister my natural sister has never been. Women like Neolitha Byrd-Johnson, Antionette Bolden, Ruby Wade, Audi Black, Milli Webb, to name a few and brothers like, Pastor Marshall Brooks, Dion Thomas, Steve Gellar, daughters like Sarah Jackson.

Know that you have a huge Spiritual family that is constantly growing and they may not always have you skin color but you all share the same blood. Even Maury would show you that.

Nevertheless, Thank God for Jesus because even in that very brief time of my son falling of course with my sister husband and friend, my continual prayers did not cease nor did God's word ever came back void.

Calvin like the prodigal son came to himself I did not even have to come or send anyone he came to himself and back to his rightful position and like the prodigal's son father I set out the party and instead of the fattest lamb he had got a Chrysler 300, and got back on his journey all because of the grace of God.

Like all children there will be times of truly Higher learning and the greater learning for the parent to learn that you are not the only influence in your child's life. I learned that even when he went away for college.

Always trust the process of God's most incredible word.

"He that begun a good work in you will perform it until the day of Christ Jesus" Phil. 1:6.

Tonya M. Thomas

Our father the Lord Jesus Christ is always true, He see's and knows everything, nothing is too big, too dark, or too hard for our God. Our children are worth the fight and patience.

With all the many accomplishments that Calvin has had from academic achievement, sports, and even government achievements, with all of his recognition he was and is even more than that.

Our children are not the sum total of what they do but who they are, embrace your children and love them for who they are not what they do or accomplish, but always remind them they are loved.

Having come from a family filled with dysfunction and uncertainty, I hadn't experienced the true meaning and expression of love. But when I saw Calvin and held him, for the first time I knew what love meant. I can only conclude that babies are the tangible grasp of the expression of God, and I'm eternally grateful that God allowed Calvin's father and me to experience that love and be the conduits of such a masterpiece. I knew when Calvin was born that he was God's choicest blessing made just for me!

This great gift unfortunately was abruptly taken from me on 11/8/12 by a drunk driver.

This drunk driver not only hit my son but he drove off, leaving my son as if he just hit an animal. It was later discovered during a trial that he alleged that he thought he had hit a **deer**, I immediately assured him he did hit what was most **dear** to me.

While my life is forever altered. I yet have been forever blessed to have shared space and time with this beautiful soul.

Am I Your Enemy Because I Tell You The Truth?

The Home-going/Celebration of life-Heaven Bound:
What brought me great comfort was first God's Holy Spirit that literally engulfed me the whole time, and the masses of support I have received from many people.

Even through his home going which for those who was in attendance have never seen anything like it. My uncle Roger Thomas said "You would have though a president died", Portions of Freeways were shut down while police escorted this very long processions.

My pastor Bishop Joseph Walker canceled his heavy schedule out of town to eulogize the home going service in over the 100 plus years of ministry there has never been a praise dance / skit at a funeral. "Take me to the King" had just came out the song was my request and was most appropriate because Calvin is and was always a "Child of the King".

During the skit a young man that had just been asked the night before during rehearsal was providentially placed, he even favored Calvin in appearance, dreads and all.

I knew I wanted this for I too, did this as a first for a great sister of mines name Antoinette Bolden for her parents' home going, I honored her parents with a liturgical dance that truly minister to the whole family this form of worship is just beyond words.

There were well over 300 people that were in attendance, they flew in, bussed, drove in, the moment they got news my house door became a revolving door from every state you can think of and from different nationalities, because to really know Calvin and I to come to our home was always comparable to going to the UN. There were people that even flew in and flew out the same day, as well as drove in to go back out the next day just to pay him homage and show me support.

What was even more beautiful the weather had an indescribable sunshine that arrayed through the skies that was beyond words.

The power of God's anointed word led by Bishop Walker provoked what both Calvin and I love most, souls to return to God, get to know him, as a result of this seed of Calvin's life it was already a mini-family reunion; many family members on both sides of his family and mines had broken relationships restored, people met their grandchildren for the first time, parents and children who had not talked were compel through the love of God to heal and forgive, marriages were healed siblings who had never met were introduced for the first time.

From Calvin' s entrance to this rim to his departure of this rim Calvin's life brought life and gave life he completed his assignment and did a Great Work, The Lord is certainly well pleased and has welcomed him with open arms.

"His lord said unto him, well done, good and faithful servant; enter thou into the joy of the Lord" Matthew 25:23

CHAPTER 9
Are You Satisfied or Pacified?

*Choose the breakthrough of the truth,
and live in an oasis of sheer bliss.*

Satisfaction Only Through Jesus Christ
When people have spent their lives pacified instead of satisfied, it's impossible for them to know the completely refreshing, thirst-quenching feeling of knowing truth and all its fruits it bears. Truth, when embrace will first make for a healthier you in your most highest form. Thereby making for healthier relationships, talents, time management, focus, purpose and fulfillment in your destiny.

There is no comparison in this earthly realm, and there is no material possession or relationship that can satisfy you in the deepest part of the yearning in your being.

Only a relationship with Jesus Christ satisfies your needs as well as your yearnings.

The outpouring of God's love and presence brings such a peace to the longings of my soul. The God of the universe loves me, cares for me, and is for me! He not only cares for me, but He cares what I care about. When I cry, He actually holds my tears in a bottle, letting me know how they are important to Him, too.

God is a refuge. He covers me when no one else will. He sustains me through every situation—ordained and not. His love takes me to heights untold.

In His hands, I am in a place free of challenges, impurities, pain, fears, doubts, worries, hurt, disappointments, letdowns, and discouragement.

I am filled with unbroken peace, weightless flows, and bounds of pure heavenly love. Stripped from the weight of people and the world, the flow of God's Spirit runs in and out of my soul like a river. His anointing bears and covers me like the sunshine in the middle of an open field. This place is home. This place is love.

When you receive God's love, you will go to heights untold. You will be endowed with His Spirit and shaped in His profound glory. This love is the purest of the pure. God's love is so vast you can't contain it, so wide you can't put your arms around it, and so tall you can't see over it. It's everywhere at all times.

The English language doesn't have fitting words to describe God's love, so there are times when all you can do is cry or just open your eyes to total amazement of the vastness of it. You can rest in it, breathe in it, sing in it, and dance in it.

Prayer Reveals Truth

There seems to be an unwritten rule that Christians should be perpetually happy people. They should never feel fear, doubt, or worry, and they should never question or challenge God. If you're like me, though, you don't view your walk of faith like that at all!

Am I Your Enemy Because I Tell You The Truth?

Imagine loosing your only son in such a way, having such a dysfunctional family, enduring a divorce, betrayals, and other horrific loses. Enduring such pains and horrific challenges one would certainly question!

From Genesis to Revelation, the Bible never says we can't question God or that we can't grow weary or frustrated. When Lazarus died, his sisters Mary and Martha prayed and believed that Jesus would come in time to heal their brother. Instead, Jesus showed up after Lazarus had been dead for several days. You can almost hear the hurt, frustration, and disappointment in Martha's voice as she told Jesus that if he had been there earlier, then her brother wouldn't have died.

The prophet Elijah showed his weariness almost immediately after one of his greatest victories. After calling down fire from heaven to prove God's mighty power to the idol god worshipers (1 Kings 18), Elijah received a death threat from Jezebel (1 Kings 19:2). Hearing this, Elijah went into the wilderness and asked God to take his life "for it is enough" (1 Kings 19:4).

Even Jesus himself, when faced with His crucifixion, prayed, "O my Father, if it be possible, let this cup pass from me" (Matthew 26:39). At times we pray and cry out to God for answers, waiting to hear something—anything—to alleviate our suffering, confusion, and pain.

Prayer reveals more than just God's answers, though. It reveals truth about God, about our situations, and about us.

In fact more than often the truth when embrace will set us up for permanent life defining moments. The greatest challenge for me is the "crazy middle." The crazy middle is when I have prayed for something and have believed with all the faith I can muster that God will grant my request. However, I hear nothing from God. Not only does it seem that He hasn't answered my prayers, but it seems as if He never even heard me.

What do you do when God is silent? What you do in those silent times reveals the truth of who you are and what you're made of.

If you're in that crazy middle now, first, take a moment to center your thoughts on what God has done in the past. Think of those times when He has answered prayer and gone above and beyond your expectations. Sometimes we have selective memory and don't recall the many times God has rescued us, protected us, provided for us, made ways, opened doors, and showered us with blessings. But in the silent seasons, that is the perfect time to recall all of those divine provisions.

Next, acknowledge that your feelings of confusion, weariness, frustration, anger, sadness, loneliness, and hurt are **real**. You don't have to pretend to be some "perfect" Christian who never gets tired, depressed, burned out, or afraid. God is big enough to handle all your feelings and so much more. As He did Job cried out when all he had had been taken from him, God heard his questions and answered him.

David said, "My tears have been my meat day and night, while they continually say unto me, Where is thy God?" (Psalm 42:3).

Am I Your Enemy Because I Tell You The Truth?

There are times when it seems all you can do is cry and wait on God while you're in your crazy middle, and you may be wondering, *Where is God?*

The truth I found in prayer helped me to see God in a different light as I waited on His answer. And while I wait, prayer has sustained me and left me with a strong sense of hope. That hope strengthened me to reject anything that wasn't in line with my expectations of what God was going to do.

Because He Went Through It, I Don't Have To

On the cross, Jesus paid all of our debts so that you and I are free in the Spirit. Knowing what Jesus did is liberating and encourages us in the faith, knowing that the wages of sin and death don't have to hang over our heads. That's the type of truth that makes us free. When I think of my heavenly Father's love, it's like a fairy tale. It is a love from another kind of place and time, and our human minds cannot conceive of such love.

Sometimes even the biblical writers struggled to articulate their feelings for God's love: "Greater love hath no man than this that a man lay down his life for his friends" (John 15:13). God's love through Jesus Christ is perfect love.

If you've ever doubted God's love for you, tell yourself as often as you need to hear it: My Father loves me! As I write this, I am in tears, but I'm not sad. My tears are of relief, awe, joy, peace, bliss, and freedom. I know that through Christ's love for me I am rescued, protected, safe, secure, satisfied, whole, and loved. I'm blown away by the fact that I didn't have to work for this love. I didn't have to earn it. I simply had to receive.

Third, know that God is talking even when it doesn't seem as if He is. He is always working even when you don't see Him doing so. God has a plan for you and is always working things out to fit that plan so that He will get the glory and so that you will have His best.

God knew Elijah was tired and hungry and feeling completely alone, so He sent a raven to feed the prophet and reassure him that God was still there and had heard him. Once fed and refreshed, Elijah could return to his journey and purpose.

Jesus knew Mary and Martha were hurt and angry over the loss of their brother, but He had a bigger purpose in mind. He wanted to show everyone there, not just Lazarus's sisters, that He is sovereign over every situation––even death.

And Jesus, though He asked the Father to let the cup of death pass, was renewed in prayer and was able to then say, "Thy will be done" (Matthew 26:42). His yielding to the Father provided salvation for countless millions of people, including you and me, which would not have been available except He offered Himself up willingly for our sins.

I know if I was to interview Job, Joseph and just to tell you about my own life and share our crazy middle. I can't ever articulate the challenges I have endured. But I can tell you that He is faithful. I nor your script is completed, He is yet unfolding his Sovereign divine plans for our lives. Rest assure that the thoughts and plans for us are good and not evil and we have an expected end.

Don't fall into the lie that it's over and it will not get any better. He alone is a comforter, my son like me, had always belonged to Him. He is the author and finisher of our Faith.

We can only hope, pray, and prepare ourselves that we finish our course He has design for our individual lives regardless of the time and age.

We must always know and remember He's Sovereign and it always in control.

So pray with confidence. Believe that God will reward you and that you will find truth in crying out to God.

Continual Transformation

Layers that keeps the larva from harm while it transforms are what I call the love of truth.

Tonya M. Thomas

If at any point in the metamorphic process the cocoon is disturbed, the larva will not develop properly and become a butterfly.

But if allowed to go through the complete transformation process the larva becomes what God intended it to be: a beautiful butterfly. Then it is able to shed its cocoon and fly free!

Many times, we try to escape our cocoon too early, or well-meaning family member or friends interrupt our metamorphic process too soon. God knows exactly how long we need to stay in our place of death, or cocoon, to produce the desired outcome. He also knows that if we don't struggle in that place, our wings will be weak and not able to carry us when its time to fly.

The metamorphic changes of life from where you are today to your unfolding journey, has oftentimes been covered ,cultivated and to the systemically designed of the lie. The encasement of the lies and distortions of the truths, ill teaching, old methodologies, and ideologies have blinded you.

Truth has come to peel back all the layers and uncover your authentic self.

God has ordained that we go through the complete process so we can be strong and able to carry out the ministry He's ordained for us.

But Don't you fear baby, because TRUTH is here, and Greater is HE that is in you than he that is in the world.

The victory has already been won and you are the Victor.

Your continual posture and position is to stay in Truth.

Am I Your Enemy Because I Tell You The Truth?

Faith is an Essential weapon to add to your arsenal!

The strategic world system, that is the source of so many dysfunctions for which you have been connected. When we get delivered from the lie we regenerate (produce and multiply the truth thereby perpetually igniting the liberty for ourselves first and then to others. From having mobileables to wearable's to implantable, the system has already began its design to release in its total form of the "LIE" (full wickedness).

Preparing the world for its ultimate goal, the "take-over" through the many devises of communication by way of technologies. These agenda are being played out daily. We are superimposed with information daily, invited or not, welcome or not ready or not. These vast masses of information are in placed to both seduced, rape and enslaved the human brain to adopt and be persuaded of its perspectives, ultimately program you for their agenda.

Please don't be deceive to believe that this will come by a hostile take-over. No in fact, it will come with kindness, pleasure, joy, through anything and anyone and will propose to you that it has your best interest in mind the whole time.

You will be totally naïve and it will blow its cover if it showed its full hand. It is in its enticement for the human soul to "need to know "always in the thirst of knowledge,"

Tonya M. Thomas

For the time will come when they will not endure sound doctrine; but after their own lusts shall they heap to themselves teachers, having itching ears; And they shall turn away their ears from the truth and shall be turned unto fables.
II Timothy 4:3-4

It will allure its captives to the slaughter of its lie to do what only it can do, that is and will always be your enemy's agenda. This is why it is most important that you stay alert and sober.

Be sober, be vigilant; because your adversary the devil, as a roaring lion, walketh about, seeking whom he may devour:
I Peter 5:8

Never underestimate the power of the lie it is not only alluring paralyzing the senses leaving you vulnerable to its assault, but it's so intoxicating consuming your ability and natural instinctive practices of the truth later leaving you a shell of a human being to make you easily pliable to further its (the lie) agenda.

Its always in incognito giving it to you in measures all while usurping all of your strength and intellect to control the ultimate (mind control) all led by your senses (what you feel, see, intellect) all limited information to keep you off focus of the (true reality).

That is why many people really do not know sometimes when they are operating in it because they have been arrested and consumed in the lie and literally are none the wiser.

Am I Your Enemy Because I Tell You The Truth?

When it is all said and done perspectives are everything your perspective is the truth on which you stand. I can give you information step by step video presentation, but if I don't break through the solid rock of your perspective I will be ineffective and you will remain the same.

You really have to cease from first your own understanding, agenda, ways, perspective, methodologies, life practices, and habits. Get into God's word that you might learn the true way, of both who you are and were intended to be. After all, with your way, will, and perspectives look where it has landed you. I know I don't have to tell you the definition of insanity "Doing the same thing yet expecting a different result".

In this truth you must remember you have come out of the darkness (light) adjust your eyes as you must but stay in the light (truth).

"Come to the light Caroline, all is welcome step into the light"- the movie *Poltergeist*.

You are going to have to learn and accept the fact that now that you are out ....you are out it is to your best interest to stay out.

You will experience rejection, become ostracize, abandoned, and the often feeling of being alone, though you are not; nor will you ever be.

"CHILDREN OF THE LIGHT, WE ARE EVERY-WHERE"-........Tonya M. Thomas.

Don't accept any part of that lie you will never be alone, that the oaky -doke, set in place in hopes for you to compromise and come

Tonya M. Thomas

back. It will often like a flirtatious woman try to lure you're back to the fold of darkness.

It will try to captivate you through your senses, you must guard your gates-(entrance to your soul) these two gates are paramount to your very soul, "the eye gate and the ear gate". Warning don't fall for the nonsense, in fact stop giving attention to insignificant people and things. I am sure if Lots wife can come back and talk to you she would warn you of the same, if the rich man (Luke 16: 19-31) can come back he will warn you of the same.

> *"Don't call this a comeback I've been here for years"*
> *LL Cool J*

You see you were here all the time the encasement of the lies and distortions of the truths, ill teaching, old methodologies, and ideologies have blinded and covered you.

When you have stepped into the place of 1st being free yourself and later freeing others the enemy (lie) would set you up to have people hating you and don't even know why others will join and don't know why they will afflict you on various levels and depths.

Some of us got in trouble not because of us anything we've done, but because of those we help. The enemy (system) has benefited with this dysfunctional system that he has set up and when you free those individuals you usurp the enemy's strength and challenge/come against-destroy his kingdom/system thereby he will send out his ranks but don't fret baby because greater is He that is in you than he that is in the world.

Am I Your Enemy Because I Tell You The Truth?

STAY SOBER GET SOBER STAY SOBER GET ALERT STAY ALERT
GET FREE STAY FREE HELP OTHERS
Forsaken
All
I
Take
Him

While I have had the privilege of **knowing God** intimately in many ways of both my son and my own life, I have by **witness** can attest to Him being **Jehovah** in our lives, He has been so mighty with His words and power in my life that all I can say is "**My Allah**", Like **Buddhism** defines He has brought immeasurable enlightenment and wisdom in my life untold.

For my brother who bought into the lie of bullet wounds, jail time, scars and tattoos have given you street credibility, or the Wars men that believe more enemies conquered and destroyed, and ranks given more stripes.   Let me tell you about the scars and stripes our Lord and Savior has already taken for you and me:

He was wounded for our transgressions, he was bruised for our iniquities; the chastisement of our peace was upon Him; and by His stripes we are healed" Isiah 53:5.

Tonya M. Thomas

He earned His stripes so we don't have to. This truth will stand regardless of what I have shared of His attributes **I will bow now**, like we all will and declare that **"Jesus is Lord"**!

"Every knee shall bow to me, and every tongue shall confess to God" Romans 14:11

Just one question... Am I your enemy because I tell you the truth?

1 Anomaly, Lecrae (Reach Records, 2014).

CHAPTER 10
Forgiveness The Final Frontier

I have chosen to share an array of my many hellacious life personal experiences . Like our heavenly father that went down to hell and took the keys from death and the grave, before reigning in all victory and power. He not only loosed himself, but He loosed others that were captured as well. I too have gone through hell and have taken some keys that has freed me and I know will free others. Out of the many keys that I have taken the key of forgiveness has been one of the most powerful.

You may be the only in your job, community, family, operating in a level of truth, causing you to be both betrayed, left for abandonment, having jealous and envious people attempt to frustrate your day. Survived a tumultuous divorce, made permanent decisions on temporary circumstances; Maybe you have suffered many major losses both naturally and tangibly. Maybe you have been on the right-side of the tracks but you were not right and cannot live up to the standard.

I will never tell you that forgiveness is easy but like the giant killer, David you too will discover that if you can survive the bears, lions, in your life then Goliath can do nothing to you. Every experience in our lives only prepares and propels us to our forward moving place in life. Forgiving my parents and sister, my x- husband, myself all have made for my bears and lions experiences. These few of my experiences, has been proofproven to exercise my internal mental and spiritual muscles that at best prepared me for coming face to face with a stranger who I didn't know or formed any bond, shared my love with, gave myself to; and forgave him for killing my only child.

What David declared even before facing Goliath was first his resume, like I and you have to do. When you have been through a lot and recognize you survived it all and are still here, that it didn't kill you that what they have done never stopped you, that the plots, plans and schemes of your haters were all ineffective. When he or her leaving you only made you better and introduce you to your destine mate.

When your loosing a job only propel you to a better job or owning your own business, when loosing your friendimies only introduced you to your real friends, when dealing with that unhealed spiritual leader only made you seek God more intimately that you discover more of him which made you need less of them, when you discover that God is Sovereign and all souls belong to Him you will never fear him who is able to kill the body but rather you will only fear Him that is able to kill both body and soul and if you and your love ones are believers you know eternity is your home and you will see each other again.

When confronting all these lies made you seek and find cover healing, freedom, resolve, refuge, in the truth. When you check out

Am I Your Enemy Because I Tell You The Truth?

your resume you will tell that Goliath (that Hellacious Trouble) "Who is this uncircumcised philistine (trouble) coming against me" (a child of the King).

My friend don't go through hell and not grab the keys......

Forgive that YOU may live :
Every disappointment, let down, backstabbers, disloyal relationships, heartaches, broken promises, racial slurs, discrimination, and pains, from people that are alive and dead.

Forgive everyone, I actually stood before the courts with standing less than 8 ft. in proximity from the guy who struck and killed my son, I didn't try to fight him, strike him, or kill him instead I released the greater power that I possess I forgave him.

The truth is Forgiveness is really for you. My forgiving my father and mother, sister, influential leaders in my life, family members, friendimies, x-husband, a vicious cycle of a divine system and the murderer who murdered my son was for me. I cannot afford to live with the cancer of unforgiveness in my heart.

I need to release what I need to receive myself and that is forgiveness. I also had to forgive myself and live. How can I profess Christianity and hate my brothers, I nor you are required to trust and put ourselves in harm ways with cantankerous relationships of any sort.

Any unhealthy relationship regardless if their maternal, work-related, or church related does not have a right in your space of life, but they are required to share the forgiveness for your place in life.

Tonya M. Thomas

The most powerful weapon for the human race is **love**. Love your enemies, treat **everyone** with respect and love, you are only required to do your part, remain consistent. God sees and knows all, He can handle all of the ill-will and practices towards you, Vengeances is His; let Him do what only He can do best.

Yes I endured the impact of having my one and only son's life taken, and like our heavenly Father does I can only do and use the power He has given me; forgive and live. There really is a release that is poured into your spirit that exchanges your anger, fear, pain, disappointment when you make the conscious choice to forgive, you literally release the power of Gods Spirit to come and overtake you. You and I cant always necessarily articulate it but I have no answer for how I can endure such horrific challenges in my life and first still be in my right mind not confront and do some harm to the individuals that intended harm towards me, this is all supernatural, His super on my natural.

Do your part and remember **you** are not **perfect,** nor did you do everything right so have grace to all human kind because we all are human beings not human become.

I can never express the difficulty of losing a child and while it is an ongoing process. I will first say seek credible Christian counseling and find a grief group that best fits you. Surround yourself with people who genuinely love and care for you. Practice and do what brings you joy, volunteer and give to others who might have experienced the same loss, Stay around joyous people that brings you laughter.

Am I Your Enemy Because I Tell You The Truth?

Take time for you, allow for the process; crying, screaming, sulking, panic attacks; it's all good. Remember all the good times and count your blessings.

I am also a nature person, I love and draw from the healing of God's creation of colorful trees ,lakes,flowers of our Great land. Apply anything or method that helps soothe your soul; from herbal tea, walks in the parks, yoga, long baths, long drives, and more importantly Gods word and His comforter, the Holy Spirit.

You possess the greatest power ,first being made in Gods Image and all that goes along with that from creativity, reproduction, having authority & dominion. Equally with that you have the power of choice. Choose wisely and always keep truth in mind. Give to others what you would like and need for yourself and that is love, patience, and forgiveness.

Remain purpose driven, kingdom-principled, and be a success oriented individual, and refuse to be distracted by Insignificant things and people. learned and you can learn as well, many things that has happened to you will and can prepare you towards your destiny Like Joseph or in my case Josephine we would have to tell our brothers "you thought/meant evil against me but God has worked it for good."

The Ultimate Truth: God Loves You!

Without God, there is no truth, and the truth of His Word that makes us free. So to know truth is to know God and to be in relationship with Him. When you know God, you can embrace His undying yet sacrificial love for you. Rest in His forgiveness and compassion, given to you without reservation and without measure.

Think about God's continual patience and enduring efforts to display His love. Imagine that the God of the universe, the Creator of all things, longs to dwell with you and share space and time and air with the beautiful and incredible you.

Despite what you've done or didn't do, God loves you. You are just that special to Him. My friend may I suggest that you meditate and received that truth!!

Am I Your Enemy Because I Tell You The Truth?

Fly on butterfly you have made it.

Forget the things that are behind; after all the caterpillar can Never go back into its encasement nor can you go back into the jail of the lies.

Truth has set you free.

ABOUT THE AUTHOR

Tonya Thomas is a native of Detroit, Michigan, and is currently living in Nashville, Tennessee. She is the proud mother of Calvin Thomas and the co-founder of C.O.K (Children of the King) Enterprises, philanthropist, and community activist, and advocate of the M.A.D.D. organization.

www.ingramcontent.com/pod-product-compliance
Lightning Source LLC
Chambersburg PA
CBHW020643300426
44112CB00007B/221